CROSSROAD

CROSSROAD

A
PILGRIMAGE
of
UNKNOWING

CHARLES MOSELEY

ὁδὸς ἄνω κάτω μία καὶ ὡυτή

The way upward and the way downward
is one and the same

Herakleitos

DARTON·LONGMAN+TODD

First published in 2022 by

Darton, Longman and Todd Ltd

1 Spencer Court

140 – 142 Wandsworth High Street

London SW18 4JJ

ISBN 978-1-913657-86-4

A catalogue record for this book is available from the British Library.

Printed and bound in Great Britain by Bell & Bain, Glasgow

Contents

Apology and Thanks

This is an untidy book, just as life is untidy, however much you pretend otherwise. Things turn up – or don't. Odd remarks challenge in ways their speaker never intended, and will never know. Words on a page in a book left lazily open on a table jump out at you and you have to answer, eventually: for most often these things work, as it were, underground, stealthily, until they surface like moles so you can no longer ignore what you must do. You take turnings you never intended when you come to a crossroads, and sometimes they lead to dead ends, and you have to go back and try again. But then, why should we expect otherwise? For life is an adventure – literally, for the word's etymology means 'chance things that happen to you.' At least, you think they are chance.

So this book is a journey, which describes remembered journeys, and as (I think) William Hazlitt remarked, travel's greatest purpose is to replace an empty mind with an open one. None of those journeys is over as yet. For the meaning of what is remembered from long ago grows as more colour goes onto the canvas, more melodic lines overlie the *cantus firmus*. Everything that comes after modifies everything that came before.

But one problem is that, with the best will in the world, on any journey you do pick up a lot of what other people might call clutter – like the bits of dried seaweed and sand-smoothed shell brought back from a child's unforgotten beach. I am particularly prone to picking up bits of information, useful or not, and dropping them into conversations and bits of writing whether people want them or not – like the Ancient Mariner's, my own poor victims cannot choose but hear. So I have taken to heart the comment of a friend who read the first complete draft of this untidy book, who chided me for 'mansplaining' lots of things that might not need it – it's a habit that comes from having been in education almost all my life. Christopher's point was warmly endorsed by my longsuffering wife Rosanna, and who can resist such a consensus? So when I felt I might be getting too informative, I have removed my digressions into the notes (or scrapped them altogether, however pleased I was with them: which is very hard to do.) You don't have to look at the notes that remain, but you can. It is rather like what they say about Confession: all can, many do, some should. That is my apology.

Now for thanks: to Rosanna, who constantly encouraged me during the writing of this book. She joined her steps to mine late in life and we explore together. (She also makes very good sandwiches for when I walk alone.) Of others directly connected with the making of this book, I am especially grateful to Christopher Catling for his wise and direct advice, to my fellow members of the community at St Mary the Less, Cambridge, and to my friends over many years in that most civilised of all Societies, that of St Mary Magdalene in Cambridge. Our friends Matthew Henderson and his wife

Enkhee, and Sarah Kotchian, on pilgrimage from the USA, understood about Iona. Then there were other people, who may never read this: a man whose name I do not know, whom I met on a remote road in Norfolk, who said more to me than he knew he did; a holy woman, Mother Catherine SSM, from the other side of the world, met by pure chance, brought me sternly to my senses when I was going nowhere after my dear first wife Jenny had died. 'You have to write', she said, and I did what my good angel said. There was a woman with wet hair, met by chance (what is chance?) in the shelter of a Dorset church while the summer storm spent its force outside, who after a conversation brief in minutes but eternal in essence, gave me a polished stone of dark marble, and a grubby piece of paper with 'Hope Renewing' written on it in pencil. I don't know who she was, or why she gave me a treasure, but her stone, which is marked with a cross crafted by some freak of ancient metamorphosis, sits on my desk as I write. I owe so much to so many people, who may not have realised that their chance remarks might have been life changing. They are too many to mention by name: but if they read this book they will know who they are. There are some, too, I can no longer thank this side of eternity – Fr John Byrom, Henry and Gillian Hart – without whom things might – would – have taken a different turn. They touched many lives besides mine. But especial thanks are due to David Moloney of Darton, Longman and Todd, without whose encouragement the book would never have appeared.

Share with me this journey from uncertainty to uncertainty, from unknowing to unknowing, all the while knowing that there is somewhere to go, someone to meet, even if our understanding is too weak to see further than the next bend in the road, our eyes are too dim to see more than the hem of a garment, our ears too dulled to hear more than the distant rumour of the music.

CWRDM

Feast of St Augustine of Hippo, Reach, 2021

1

To begin with...

I have always been a walker – not in the old heroic mode, however. For there was a time in the earlier twentieth century when dons from Cambridge, even elderly ones like me, would walk to London in a single day. One of those elderly dons, an old and dear friend of mine, used to walk at least once each year from Rosthwaite in Borrowdale to climb Scafell Pike, Helvellyn, and Skiddaw between a midsummer moonrise and the next sunset. My style was gentler, my ambitions more modest, and I think some with whom I have walked thought me a bit of a wimp. No matter: my walks in the high hills of these islands, along coasts of airy cliff or yielding shingle, over the springy machair of a holy island, or across the green heart of England, were rich enough at their time, and they got richer as onto my own memory, reading and knowledge, the experience and thought and memory of others was grafted to bear unexpected, and grateful, fruit.

But memory is not a simple thing, involuntary. For St Augustine it was, with Reason and Will, one of the three parts of the soul. John Donne, in a sermon on Psalm 38 given at

11

Lincoln's Inn around 1620, connects it intimately with salvation. For the ancients, remembering was an art – Memory constructs, interprets, changes. And I know mine works differently as I get older. Once it was effortless to recall both the important and the utterly trivial with precise exactness. But now … I used to get so irritated with myself when I could not remember, say, who had held what office in whose Ministry, or a date, or a reference to a piece of scholarship, or quote accurately, or recall what Haber's Process was all about. But now I think, does it really matter? Does it really matter that I have forgotten things I once knew – or perhaps more accurately, that my neural pathways to those spots where they are stored have got overgrown, as untrodden ways do? Does it matter that I can no longer cite chapter and verse at the drop of a mortar board, remember accurately a bibliographical reference, or tell you which of all those Saxon nobles and ladies beginning in 'Aeþel-' was which, and from where and with whom? No: what matters is how that knowledge has been distilled into a way of seeing, thinking, and, one hopes, understanding. You don't look for the golden grain or the blue berries of the juniper in the gin, but you do enjoy its clarity and the power they made possible. Perhaps this might relate to something St Paul says in 1 Corinthians 13:8: 'Charity never faileth: but whether there be prophecies, they shall fail; whether there be tongues, they shall cease; whether there be knowledge, it shall vanish away.' But I don't think he was thinking of gin.

This book had to be written: it forced itself on me. It recalls, describes, to be sure, some of my own journeys on foot, but more importantly it is about what those walks have come to mean, as I remember them – and that process of understanding is certainly not finished. Thinking about the past to me is rather like letting light into dusty corners of a neglected room: it's a way of understanding where I might have got to on the journey, and sometimes it provides the impetus for the next step – even if where it is taking me is still uncertain. (I shall not know until I cannot speak of it.) As (I think) William Faulkner said, 'The past isn't dead, it isn't even over.' It makes present and future. I hope that what I say may be of some help to others stumbling along on their own uncertain journeys. Mine, I can now see, were all one walk, indeed, each going through time and space and place to the beginning of another, and the Road goes ever on, even though my day is far spent and the night is at hand.

2

Up The Helm

O thou that tellest good tidings to Zion,
get thee up into the high mountain.
Isaiah 40:9

'Once upon a time' – all good stories begin like that, but
that does not mean this will be one – there was a man called
Kraki. We know virtually nothing about him: he was born, he
was a man probably of some substance, he died. But he has left
a mark on the land he might have called his own. Where two
long roads cross he set up a Cross. The paths he knew are now
thin tarmac roads deep cut into the landscape between high
hedges, so unfrequented that grass grows in the middle. They
were already ancient ways when Kraki's people came to that land
from the deep fjords and high fjells of Norway. And ever since
he set up his cross, the scattered hamlet that grew up on that
clayey drumlin country east of the noisy gorge of the capricious
Kent has been known as Crosscrake. What the earlier people
who trod the ancient roads called it we know not, nor who they
were. Sometimes you stumble over things they left behind, and
in some places ... well.

Just behind the church a steep little churchyard snuggles
into the angle of the crossroad. In season it is a joyful riot of the
wildflowers which I knew as a boy in those lanes, when I visited
my 'uncle' Alec, the Vicar – he was my father's close friend –
who lived in the big slate-built vicarage on the top of the hill
a half mile away: a long way for my little child's legs. If I stood
there, as I often did, where Kraki's cross probably stood, and
looked north and a bit east towards Kendal, I could see the top
of The Helm. It is only a little hill, but it matters, for it is the
first I ever wanted to climb ('because it was THERE'). I used to
long to climb it, and never knew why, and did climb it one day
with Margaret. She was five years older than me, and had pigtails
I never dared pull, and was always ahead. I remember we had
Hector the white Scottie belonging to my uncle and 'aunt' (and
Margaret), with us, who ran in front and started the odd rabbit
out of shelter. He was too fat ever to have a chance of catching
one. I thought the walk, now we were doing it, very steep and
a very long way. The late summer bracken was almost as high
as my five year old head, and I could see a litter of old bracken
from years before on the ground beneath the colonnade of the
brown stems. I remember I was lagging and hot and grumpy,
and then we came out to a sudden sight of all the kingdoms of
the world, it seemed, spread out below us. (Ever after, when
Uncle Alec preached on the Temptations, I imagined Jesus on
The Helm looking down at Kendal and then turning to look over
to the distant Irish Sea.) And I could see beyond it higher hills
and yet higher hills, which called to me: one satisfied desire leads
only to another unsatisfied one. As the years passed and the clear
domain of childhood receded into the blue rumour of memory, I
drove past that hill many times on my way to somewhere else in

cars far, far faster than the maroon and black Vicarage Morris 8, and then the grey Morris E type. Plump Auntie, blue straw hat pinned to the bun of her black hair streaked with lines of silver, drove her quiet little husband to meetings, singing hymns at the top of her considerable voice. He did not sing: he could intone the service, but, well, *bleated* in that once common Anglican manner.

The Helm was always there. It was one of those fixed points on my young horizon, like the warm homeliness of Crosscrake.

And then, for reasons that I do not really know, knowing nobody anymore in a place where once everyone knew me – long years away had separated me from that time – as I was driving on my way to somewhere else I came to the crossroads, on an impulse turned off on a road long not travelled, and went up that path to The Helm again. Something made it necessary. No Margaret this time: she died young, long ago. My companion this time was young and black and comely, and delighted to be out and about with me at a time when the flowers appear on the earth, the time of the singing of birds is come, and the voice of the turtle is heard in our land. Hector was a Labrador of noble lineage, and it was impossible not to share his delight at being out on a grand day with lots of new smells (for him), it was impossible not to begin to shake off the melancholy and lassitude that had been bugging me for weeks. We came out onto the long summit, into the light dappled by the scudding fair weather cumulus clouds that the stiff breeze was pushing off the sea.

There is a hill fort – Iron Age, but people would have used this commanding hill long before that was built. It may be that those folk who made the lanes by Kraki's Cross used it. Its rampart and ditch make a sinuous circuit of the hill. We walked it, of course. And saw nobody. There were larks, and a kestrel, Hopkins' windhover, trod the wind before off, off, forth on swing to another station where the keen eyes could scan the ground for movement that might mean food. A rabbit excited Hector as it bolted into the bracken nearby. Hector looked at me expectantly: 'Please?' 'No,' I said firmly, and gave him a biscuit. On the top I sat down, and looked over to the line of the Kent marked by the trees along its bank, and far over to the Lakeland hills beyond, blue with distance. Hector does not like it very much when I stop and sit down, and flumped down with a sigh beside me. It was easy to fall into a reverie, thinking about the people who built this fort. Is it something as simple as that, in fact, or something much more complex? I don't know. Perhaps they enjoyed being up here in the sun and wind as much as I realized I do, even had their place of assembly, possibly even of pilgrimage and worship, up here. (High places have always been special to humankind, it seems: and in ancient Israel the Baalim had their ritual places on the tops of hills, but, says the Psalmist, in Psalm 121, damn all help came from *them*.[1]) They can't really have lived here for very long, with their animals, because, as with so many hill 'forts' (a word which begs so many questions), there is no adequate supply of water. But as I began to doze, to go into

[1]   I am going to be pedantic – probably not for the last time. St Jerome's translation of the Psalms into Latin made the opening 'Lev*avi* oculos', 'I *lifted* up my eyes unto the hills', which is firmly past tense, and one assumes he knew his Hebrew (a language where tenses are sometimes problematic anyway). Coverdale's English translation made it present: the Anglican Book of Common Prayer, despite quoting Jerome's Latin at the beginning, makes it future: 'I *will* lift up...' Which is why the psalm is so often part of the funeral services for hill walkers and climbers. By the vagaries of translation the ancient poem has gained a resonance of which its author could never have conceived.

what I call the mind's soft focus, I fancied – not for the first time – that I could hear the Old Ones' voices in the wind, that if I turned round I would see them, that they were not gone, that the place remembered them. They have left no names, as Kraki did. But they were there. They called this place their own – if they had any concept of 'owning' things. And they were, unquestionably, our ancestors, our family.

When I am on the point of sleep I have a recurrent – well, not a dream exactly, but something more mysterious. Sometimes I will go many months without it happening; sometimes it is almost every night. I seem to be looking into a place I feel I ought to know, but don't. It is a monochrome world, and there are people. They are not people I know, but I see them in sharp, even intimate, detail, the very wrinkles round the eyes and the marks of a bad shave, and they seem to see me looking at them, and look me in the eyes and seem to try to speak, but I hear no sound. Their clothes are not modern, but not ancient either. They are not the clothes people wore when I was a lad, but older than that. And I can stir myself and describe their features in detail to my wife, who actually is, most often, asleep. But she finds this inconclusive, puzzling experience intriguing, for it seems to relate to her own – well, memory? – of other lives. It seems to matter, as if some sort of connection is being made between me now and they – then? But what are 'now' and 'then'? We are so trained to thinking of events as occurring on a linear timeline, where something distant on that timeline is also distant from us. But it is not the only way to think: I am told that the Sami, for example, think of event as indelibly linked to place, and in a place we are near that event, no matter when it happened. So places hold stories.[2] Even in our own supposedly materialist culture this way of seeing may be more common at some levels than we think. For I remember old people in my father's village who had little sense of a past behind their own and their parents' generation, of a past linearly extended through the long arches of the years, a perspective into worlds circling different suns. What mattered to them was the Now time, the *jetztzeit*. That meant that stories of the critical, scarring, events of long ago were as if only yesterday. What happened during the Civil War, say (with the legacy of which we still live), could have happened only a day or two ago. In Talke, the village where my father was born, they told me, then an earnest lad in short trousers who asked questions, that the next village, Red Street, was called that because the road ran with blood 'after the soldiers came': their parents had told them, and it might have been yesterday rather than three centuries back. To see otherwise, to see the past as a perspective is a skill that has to be learned, and when I was about nine I certainly had not even begun to develop that. For example, Mum revered the memory of her adored father, often talked about him, and quietly hoped, I am sure, I would be a scholar and parson like him. She once said to me, thoughtfully, 'He was a saint, you know'. And I knew his name was Charles, and I could not fit him into the Twelve, so I assumed he must have had another name (like Peter), and said, 'Which one?'

[2] Not a bad example, even if oversimplified, of this can sometimes be glimpsed in placenames. On Tristan da Cunha there is a spot on a cliff called 'Place Where The Goat Jump Off'. On Iona the little bay of Port na Curragh got – that name it surely had one before that – from the momentous landing there of a leather boat with a banished and repentant prince and 12 companions.

What called me to walk up The Helm with Hector for that first time in well more than half a century? What calls me back from time to time to certain spots in the lanes at Crosscrake where the pignuts grew, or the wild strawberries, or to the (now drained) canal at Stainton, to the cool stillicide – cool on the hottest of days – where busy St Sunday Beck rushes in its dark, echoing, stone vault under the Canal? Why do I want to show them to the people I especially love, knowing (as I do) they can mean nothing, carry no memories, for them? But going there with them, telling them your story in that place, can give them a rich gift. The happiest photo I have of my mother, who had had much trouble and sorrow in her life, was when, at her suggestion, we had driven her, then well on in years, on a day trip to New Brighton. She had not been for over sixty years, but that afternoon she saw not how different the place now was, with the bombing of a war, the devastation of recession, and the jerrybuilding of the 1960s, but was walking with the ghosts of her beloved mother and father and her dead siblings, recalling the annual exchange of city parish – poor parsons like my grandfather could not afford holidays – for duty in a seaside church. She was recalling how they ate shrimps in conical brown paper bags on the beach as a treat, how there was a uniformed band playing on the bandstand, how her mother played the organ at the (now redundant) church – the organ was sounding in her head as she talked of that church – and how they tried to persuade the stubbornly silent parrot of the holidaying incumbent to talk. (Since we are speaking of memory, that parrot had a remarkable and exact one, in fact. The children heard later that their teaching had been a success, for the bird welcomed its owner back with a bravura aria, *fortissimo,* of all the swear words which they had heard in the streets of Oldham. Ever after, its cage had to be covered up whenever visitors were expected.) You don't always want people, or birds, to tell you what they remember. Nor do they want to, always, but can't always help it. But what I know is that Mum gave me her memories, and they have somehow subtly become mine when I think of that place to which I shall never go again. Her gift expanded in the giving.

+ + +

One day when late summer was turning into Autumn, one of my dearest friends and his brother, both now dead, took me miles along the shifting, sounding shingle of a Norfolk beach back to their childhood. The two men seemed to find the hard going less tiring to their elderly thighs than I did to my much younger ones. But then, they were used to it: when boys they had spent summer after summer on a boat moored where the shingle spit then ended and finally allowed the little river to mingle its waters with the sea.

The *Yankee* had begun life as a humble little coaster, carrying cargoes, as they came along, between the now quiet harbours around the Wash. She had come pretty much to the end of her economic life by the end of the First World War, and had retired to be a houseboat, moored in the shallow water inside the spit. The water left her on spring ebbs, and did so more and more as the silts built up over the years. The family had a couple of little dinghies, Norfolk flatties, single masted with a lug sail, that a young lad of ten or so could handle well enough to go safely across the estuary at slack water on the top of the tide to get milk and things from the shop in the village: much quicker than the two hours and more of walking right round. At each low tide when the estuary emptied, the banks of shining mud were noisy with feeding birds, with the piping of oystercatcher and redshank, and the harsh 'kria' of the terns — some call them sea-swallows. On the storm beach the ringed plovers made their invisible nests and in the dunes you might — still can sometimes — see a harrier. When, each summer's end, the family padlocked the door, dropped the key off at the shop in the village, and left for another academic year, the first wintering geese would be beginning to arrive from the high North.

Times change. Families fly off to different nests of their own. Wartime comes again, when the spit becomes once more a restricted area. Only men in khaki uniform, keeping uneasy watch for what might come from the sea, join the birds and rabbits in the wind off the North Sea. The *Yankee* settles a little more comfortably into the mud, and only the highest tides of equinox with a northerly behind them now shift her slightly. The fine sand blows along the shore and in big storms forms dunes that slowly march westward, ever westwards, taking the spit to far, far beyond where the high tide once raced round the point and on the ebb left the low flats where the seals could bask. The *Yankee's* woodwork decays or is scavenged for campfires, her iron ribs grow dark brown and swell with rust. But she is still recognisably a boat. For a time.

I followed the two men as they climbed over the dune, and looked down, across the shining low tide mud, with the silver channel of the river snaking in the middle. At their feet the few ribs stuck up through the marram grass and silverweed. You could see there had been a boat there. By her stern the marsh plants, shrubby sea blight (*sueda vera*), sea lavender, sea aster, sea purslane take over and wade out to where the water often comes. Rabbit scrapes in the sand, and rabbit droppings, show how busy the place is when we are not looking. Dry whitened shells, bits of shelly crab legs on patches of close-nibbled grass hint at the feasting of birds. There is a tide mark of brown grass stems and bits of blackened seaweed. The tiller still pretends it directs the boat as she points into the dunes. The two old boys move around the wreck, talking happily about where things were, about the time before … about their parents, their father correcting examination papers all summer day long, to be taken eventually to the railway station in the village and sent back to the University: and they talk about their brother, accidentally shot dead on a wildfowling trip when a boat suddenly lurched. One of them stands at the tiller, as once he did before. But she won't answer their helm anymore. At least, not in a time I can get to.

We ate our sandwiches, sitting on the dune above the wreck. The brothers were quiet as ghosts, hearing undead voices in another wind. One smoked his ancient pipe, silent, looking at the past. But soon the wind blew cold, and the sun was going down. Time to go, soon.

Why did Henry and Norman take me along those bitter-sweet miles of shingle to show me the wreck? A man I revere, who taught me much more than he thought he did, once wrote that perhaps in Heaven he would be able to take his friend on a walk round all his favourite childhood spots in the sweet country of County Antrim – drumlin country too, like that round Kendal, as it happens. But, for now, you can't resurrect the people and animals you knew, or introduce them to new friends, however much you want to. They have gone from this age of the world.

You know that the place to which you go back will always have changed – sometimes so radically that only little fragments remind of what used to be there, like the bare rotting ribs of the beloved houseboat just poking through the engulfing sand as the long sigh of the tide draws back. You know you cannot see with the eyes you had years ago. You are yourself a ghost: you knew the place, the people, so well, and nobody now knows you. But I know that when I go now, alone, trudging along the shingle to watch the seals on the point, those two boys, both now dead, sailing their flatties, and the slow lift of the *Yankee* as the tide makes, and the kettle beginning to sing on the coal stove, are, in my memory, *now* as if I had been there then. They are as real as was the scent of tobacco from that villainous pipe, blown away on the wind from the sea. The presentness of the past is in all I see: sometimes more real than the actual.

So what is it that draws you to return to a place in fact or in memory, or to journey to a new place where others have already *told* something of what you will hold as memory? Is it a desire to – shall we say? – reboot? To touch base with where you seem to remember you were happy? To go back to a time before the choices, and choices, and choices – not all our own – made problematic Now inevitable? What were the other once-possible scripts, scenarios? Is it a longing for a simplicity you lost when the child ceased, ever so subtly, to be childlike? Or is it – it could be all of these of course – a sort of pilgrimage more or less consciously made to the ancient powers that once guided, guarded perhaps, your little world and set up the mould by which you still judge reality, consciously or not? Or where you might find a sort of unison in the discord of conflicting voices in which we live day to day, and go forward with new understanding? Is the end of all our travel an arrival where we started, knowing the place for the first time? Or – and more and more I come to think this is a clue to the answer – is our return to the loved places like swinging the compass on a boat about to go to sea, so that you will have a true bearing for the voyage ahead over unpathed waters to undreamed shores?

'I will arise, and go now' ... It's not a sterile nostalgia, however many bean rows you might plant in your idyll.[3] Part of what draws you to return in fact or in memory is the wish to think and write honestly about people and places you love. So many people over the ages, and now, have felt, have written about, that restlessness: here is no abiding City, here is not our real *heimat*, here is no eternal stay. No indeed: man is not just *sapiens* – would he were indeed wise! – but *peregrinus*, a traveller, for good or ill. James C. Scott,[4] and others, have argued, very powerfully, that our species' ills, from politics to taxes to epidemics, stem in large measure from settling, abandoning hunting and gathering, and the cyclic change of place as the seasons warm and cool, in favour of agriculture six or so thousand years ago – a blink of an eye ago. And the effects on our planet have hardly been wholly benign. I honestly think it is against our deepest nature as a species to be settled, and if by choice or perforce, if we

---

[3] Nothing ever was an idyll, really – as was soon clear when we first came to this village, then a remote spot, where I write. It was seething with old resentments, the winter mud clogged your feet, the house was bitterly cold, and the Seven Deadly Sins had – were! – local colour. It was not, is not, a museum of sentiment with wistful ponies (let's be anthropomorphic) leaning over gates to have their ears rubbed, while cheery old men sit in the sun outside the pub with a pint. I had hopes of being one of those myself, once upon a time.

[4] *Against the Grain: A Deep History of the Earliest States* (2017).

actually *do* stick in the mud, we are often disgruntled, tetchy, quarrelsome. It is our nature to travel, in time as well as space, in memory as well as in expectation, and those who came before us blazed the trail for us. St Augustine of Hippo put that beautifully: 'By travelling the narrow road they widened it, and went ahead of us, trampling down the rough ways as they went along'.[5] We are doing the same. We make the road for others by walking it, and the journey is what we are made for.

I suppose my own restless going up The Helm that bright day was a sort of pilgrimage to a sunny memory of kindliness and kindly — lovely word! — people. But it was not a running away from some grey and drear present, for despite the knocks Dame Fortune gives us, I have had an interesting and full life and there is still plenty to do while time lasts — like writing books … and hoping that somebody will read them and say, 'Gosh, me too!'

I think what drives me, and others with whom I have shared these thoughts, is sensing a sort of incompleteness, where the pressure of the linear melody of the present does not allow for the polyphony where many voices, dead and gone and only now just tuning up, can sing together. To be able to introduce those well remembered to those well loved now; to be able to hear the ancient voices in the ancient chancel they sang in when it was new, as our choir gets ready for another challenge Jeff the choirmaster is setting us — well, that would be something. And to be able to say to the old ones whose world circled a different sun, 'It's all right, we think. How was it for you?'

And so I have come to love, and seek out, old places, old nodes of the world where people have gone for centuries. There

[5]   Augustine of Hippo, *Sermon* [306B] *for the feast of Saint Quadratus.*

are places – islands, hills, springs – places apart, where time drops away, and where, if you go quiet, you can feel a different rhythm. Was The Helm a place people called holy, once? And what do we mean by holy? George MacLeod, who founded the Iona Community, called Iona 'a thin place where only tissue paper separates the material from the spiritual'.

There are many such places, when thought falls silent and only a luminous be-ing remains. We each need to be quiet, and go into that desert. It is not far away.

3

OLD PATHS

'Stand ye in the ways, and see, and ask for the old paths,
where is the good way, and walk therein,
and ye shall find rest for your souls.
But they said, 'We will not walk therein.'
Jeremiah 6:16

O nce,[6] alone and silent, I walked across England to where the sun sets below the rim of the restless western sea. I could not, even now, say why, exactly. Sometimes a starling in a winter murmuration needs to leave the great dance of everyday, fly its own path, in order to know its place as the dance resumes. Perhaps that walk on my own was connected – but not consciously – with several coincident watersheds of our lives: first, our son leaving home and the nest now empty. The lad – I envied him – was going off far faring in icy lands where the summer sun never set, lands I had known and loved and would know again (but I saw no

---

[6]   An earlier, and very much shorter, version of the next few pages appeared in my *Hungry Heart Roaming: An Odyssey of Sorts* (London: Black Spring/ Eyewear, 2021), to which this book is loosely a sequel. There is a lot of walking in that one too.

chance of that then; life is always throwing unexpected things at you). Then there was a massive job change of gear for my wife, and the final, expected but dreaded winding down for me of a major job I had loved doing. It all came at once. It was a time when we both realised we needed to have time apart in order to be together. What do we do next? Where do we go from here? We talked about it, but shyly, tentatively, for it meant admitting to each other and ourselves that we had got quite a lot wrong: it's a feeling many of us have at some point in our lives, and it isn't comfortable, and some couples don't weather it. It can be a time when something makes you realise that life is not a straight line, it doesn't behave as you thought you had planned it. Fr Richard Rohr[7] puts it well: in the first stages of life we are dependent, learning the ropes, how to survive being human among humans. That morphs into what he calls the 'Young Warrior' stage – the stage when you are doing things, confidently showing (off) who you are (or like to think you are), making your mark (as they say), piling up achievements, honour, or a fortune: a character that others recognise. Then (and sometimes this is devastating), you realise that what you thought mattered to you on your first journey as Young Warrior actually doesn't matter much at all, and, more disconcertingly, that nobody has really noticed anyway. What is it all about? Sometimes it takes what looks like disaster – divorce, illness, unemployment, bereavement – to your norms to make you realise that you've seen enough of your own tricks and posturing to know that that is what they are, and that they are not what you *really* are. But a lot of the things you had thought did not matter now do matter very much indeed.

[7]   *Falling Upward: A Spirituality For The Two Halves Of Life* (2013).

Some people never get beyond the Warrior stage, and you can never predict when – if – the watershed between the two halves of life will happen – younger in some than in others, but for some perhaps never. Some get there, to the watershed, and find the view down the opposite slope too terrifying, and turn back. I think of pitiable old men still obsessed by success, by piling up a fortune they do not need and could never enjoy; I think of the drug of power and status from which the withdrawal is too awful to contemplate. In this second journey other imperatives take over: the search for understanding, recognition that your own vision is only a part of the great Vision, the paramount importance of a love that grows by being given away, the recognition and even joyful acceptance of the mortality the young never think belongs to them. But each of those grand things demands of us a painful humility – and that is much, much easier to 'know about' than to do. There is an art in getting ready to leave just as there is in knowing how to join the party.

That first difficult summer on our own – what do parents talk about when the nest is suddenly empty and the bathroom free and the phone bill less? – we were set to go to Northumberland for a long weekend break, but traffic on the A1 led to a diversion, and then I made a mistake at a crossroads, and then we found ourselves on the wrong road and then – why not? – decided it was the right one. From that chance decision – but what is chance? – grew the idea of crossing England from sea to shining sea, as the cliché has it, and that fitted perfectly with a long-standing, indeed growing, curiosity about what life at two and a half to three miles per hour might feel like, if only for a few days. On top of that was the recognition that until the nineteenth century walking was how most people, my ancestors indeed, got about. What did it feel like for them? I'd so like to ask them, share what they cannot tell me. And how might your vision change? After all, when you have spent years teaching something, like the practice and importance of travel and pilgrimage in mediaeval culture and religion, you do get curious about what it might feel like from the inside — like actually trying out mediaeval recipes rather than just being knowledgeable about them. (Some of which are really quite good, if rather sweet for my taste.) Having so often *said* things about faith, something was challenging me to do more: actually to see whether I believed what I had taught. You have to make that journey alone.

Our wrong turning had us ending high up on a cliff above a small village, looking out over the grey waters of the North Sea and flooded Doggerland. New country. Neither of us knew it, or had any associations with it. Some symbolism there ...

+ + +

We found somewhere to stay — alas, it was vegetarian, and I do like my bacon and eggs and black pudding for breakfast — and over two days we walked the coast. From pretty Staithes, sheltered from northeasters by the headland that turns the beck south where it runs into the sea, to the long sands of Whitby and the ruins of the Abbey on the southern headland was one day; then from Whitby over Ravenscar, where once was one of Rome's chain of signal stations, to busy Scarborough and a bus, noisy and crowded with home-going children, back to where we had left the car. At Runswick Bay a shuttered café, with wind-drift of blown sand against its doors, made us glad we had brought something to eat with us. We sat at the edge of the marram grass fringing the beach with our sandwiches, the little dune supporting our backs. The dry sand at our feet stirred in the wind off the sea. The sharp points of the hard-edged blue-green grass blades, arched over and touching the soft sand, scribed ceaseless little arcs. The returning sea sang us a song of slow somnolence, as each wave fell on the beach and drew back with a lingering sigh. It was quite hard to get up, to shoulder our light packs, and set off again.

We climbed out of Whitby up to the ruin of the Abbey, the wind sounding through its empty windows. Though this once grand stone building long postdates the (probably wooden) double monastery of monks and nuns founded in 657 by Oswy, king of vast Northumbria, it is the sort of place where you hear echoes, voices, in the wind: I could not *not* feel the importance of that argument, and decision, at the Synod Oswy called seven years later, on this spot whither I had never planned to come. Which I had only read about and thought about.[8] Nor could I forget the thrill I felt as a

---

[8] In 664 King Oswy (or Oswiu) called the Synod of Whitby, about which I remember Miss Murphy telling us when we were in the top class at Beach Road County Primary School, to settle a growing problem: the Celtic, or Irish, church – the parent of Lindisfarne and a hugely energetic missionary church – differed in many of its practices from the Roman church. (St Augustine's mission, the initiative of Pope Gregory the Great, had successfully been established in 597 in Kent and was followed by Paulinus' in parts of the north after 625.) The new abbey was governed by Hild, of the royal house, who had been called by Aidan of Lindisfarne to the religious life.

The Celtic and Roman churches differed in many ways and the Synod sought to resolve the problems these caused. One was the date of Easter: the Celtic church, claiming the authority of St John's Gospel, held it on the fourteenth day of the Jewish New Year (the date of the Crucifixion) which did not always fall on a Sunday; Rome, after the decision at the Council of Nicaea in 325, held that it must be on a Sunday, that the Jewish tradition did not bind Christians, and that it should fall on the first Sunday after the first full moon after the Spring Equinox. As Easter determines the whole liturgical year, this difference mattered: for example, Oswy, baptised in the Celtic tradition, had

student when the Old English of Caedmon, the first English poet of whom we have knowledge, began to make sense to me, its rich sounds and patterns resonating in my mind into a hymn of wonder and praise. He was the Abbey's cowherd, who was given the gift of poetry – and poets had high status in Anglo Saxon England, as they did in Ireland – and became a zealous monk.[9] He was here when

one date for the Easter feast, while his queen Eanflaed, who had been brought up in the Roman tradition, was still deep in the fast of Lent. But the issues were wider: at bottom was the issue of whether the authority of Rome would take precedence over the looser organisation and slightly different rites of the Irish. Wilfrid, the abbot of Ripon, whose training had been in part at Celtic Lindisfarne before he went to Canterbury and Rome, (his stone throne is still in Hexham Abbey and once I sat in it), argued the case for the Roman, and Bishop Colman of Lindisfarne for the Celtic tradition. Famously, Oswy asked, 'Who is the gatekeeper of heaven?' Everyone could agree on St Peter, and the Popes claimed to be his successors. It was to Wilfrid the King deferred.

It all sounds so academic and remote, fit only for a footnote. But on that decision the whole future development of Church and State in Britain took a new and decisive direction: to what we are NOW. That is not to say that something valuable was not lost, which many are now painstakingly trying to recover.

[9] I loved Caedmon's poem, so here it is, with a bit of the Venerable Bede's information thrown in. Bede says Caedmon was a cowherd, who, at feasts in the hall, when people would take turns singing to the harp, would get up when he saw the harp getting close to where he sat, and go to his cattle shed. But he had a mystical experience there in which he was given a calling to sing: first of all, about Creation:

> *Nu sculon herian heofonrices Weard,*
> *Metodes mihte and his modgeþanc,*
> *weorc Wuldorfæder, swa he wundra gehwæs*
> *ece Dryhten, or onstealde.*
> *He ærest scop eorþan bearnum*
> *heofon to hrofe halig Scieppend.*
> *þa middangeard mancynnes Weard*
> *ece Dryhten, æfter teode*
> *firum foldan Frea ælmihtig.*

the Synod decided that the church in what was not yet England must be focussed on Rome rather than Ireland. I am glad I have looked out from the headland at the waters he saw and heard his words in my head. I shall not pass that way again.

From the headland we could see over the leaden sea that the horizon was vague, misty: perhaps a sea roke coming in. Better that than the *drakkar* of the Viking raiders who came out of the dawn in 857 and destroyed the monastery ... When their ships had been sighted before, they had been coming in peaceable trade. Its ruins on the deserted site sang only the songs the wind taught until the Normans refounded it in 1078. Better the roke, too, than the two German cruisers that December morning in 1914, whose shells hit what Henry VIII's Commissioners had left in 1539 after their usual wrecking job.

The roke came rolling in, damp and wet, not very thick but with a chill in it. Everything was suddenly indistinct. Ahead of us a foghorn started booming, pulse regular and identifiable to those who knew the code. Some sort of a symbol there for the journey this walk became? Perhaps. The lighthouse when we came to it surprised by its squatness. One expects lighthouses to be straight and tall, but of course, if they are on a cliff ....

By the time we dropped down steeply into Bay Town our hair was damp, our jackets beaded with moisture. We could not see much. Might it be a good idea to stop now? No, one does not do that ... so, a brisk pace along the beach at the edge of the

(Now Him let us praise, who holds heaven's kingdom, the might of the maker and the marvels his mind conceived, all this fashioning, the wonders, by the father of glory, Lord eternal, wrought in the beginning. First heaven He shaped as roof for the children of men, then mankind's guardian made Middle Earth — the eternal Lord, almighty King, adorned the earth for living creatures.)

tide, just the few discernible tired-looking little waves coming out of the muffler of fog and exhausting themselves running up the tiny incline of the sand. On we went, past slumping soft cliffs of glacial till atop shales, mudstones and sandstones laid down in warm, unimaginable seas where squid-like belemnites and nautilus-like ammonites swam. I found a fossil belemnite: they are not uncommon. The stone is a print, a hard ghost, of what was once a living thing of beauty. I threw it away: after all, extra weight, and I have pots of them in the Cabinet of Curiosities at home. We climbed up to Ravenscar, and the roke lifted just as we made the top, and in sunlight we could see the way we had come and far out over the grey sea. Exhilaration of a sort ... From here the Romans watched for the raiders from the east ... Was that when the daft idea crystallised: why not walk, but alone, to the other sea that faced the sunset? 'If you wish, if it feels right for you,' she said, with that generosity on which, without knowing it, I relied so much.

Once you have had an idea in you that challenges something – who knows what? – it is difficult to put it down. It kept nudging me, and in the end I thought, without a lot of enthusiasm, I might as well do it. Jenny continued to raise no objection. I could make enough time free that summer to do at least a half of it, and could finish it later. Perversely – yet not quite so, for I felt I ought to get my muscles fit for the highest hills – I chose to do the traverse east to west, into the prevailing weather rather than having it at my back. There was rather a lot of weather, especially in the long stretch crossing the Pennines to the Lakes, almost an Empty Quarter in a crowded England. I saw hardly anyone, talked to fewer. I camped some nights in the shelter of ancient walls with only Rough Fell or Swaledale sheep within earshot, sometimes finding a bed and breakfast so that I could wash. Not that washing did much good.

As far as I could, I avoided roads and followed old, empty ways, packhorse way, overgrown footpath, drove way, corpse way – much easier when you get into the wilder parts. Some parts of the journey have left little in the way of memory: much of the first half must have been plain dull. Between the coast where the idea had first claimed me and the day I found myself looking down on the English Heritage-manicured ruins of Rievaulx Abbey nothing much of interest comes back. Of later, a trudge along the hedged lanes crossing the lush soft farmland – modern industrialised farms, smelling sometimes of chemicals – of the Vale of Mowbray, with the smudge of the Pennines on the western horizon, I remember more what I thought about than what I saw. One field was very like another and there was not much weather to complain about. There was the roar of the A1 to be crossed – a boundary as divisive as any river. Once we called it the Great North Road; to the locals it was Leeming Lane. That road, probably older than the Romans, led to the huge earthworks a few miles north of the Brigantian capital of Stanwick – couldn't help thinking about Cartimandua and how she supported the Romans against her husband Venutius! – placed to command one route going north to the Lothians and the other going west over Stainmore to Carlisle and the West. (Alas, being on my own I could not explain that to anyone.) That junction saw conflict more than once, for by either route came the raiding Scots, or before them the men of Gododdin or Rheged, or the men of Man. Aneirin's elegy for the defeat of the flower of the men of Gododdin and Gwynedd by the Angles of Bernicia and Deira – soon to be Northumbria – about 600 at somewhere called Catraeth (probably Catterick) is one of the earliest Welsh poems, plangent in its expression of loss, of grief, of pride in the fallen. It has one of the earliest mentions of the mysterious Arthur, but it could have been written in the grief after any war, any battle, any old, forgotten strife. When I first came across it, its web of allusion and pattern made reading it difficult, like cutting through a thorn hedge. But it was worth it: I could feel in my stomach, in a sort of excitement, 'This matters: this is ancient sorrow. People like you might have to be, one day, in a world this uncertain.'

Scotch Corner: how prosaic, dull! a fitting name for what is now a dull place with a dull hotel!

Later, returning after a spell when work and duty had kept me down south, I paused, drew breath, at Richmond before setting off on the journey that would not physically end till I reached the sea. (I found a very good pork pie shop just off the marketplace.) Some say Arthur and his knights are sleeping under the hill of Richmond's Norman castle till Britain shall have dire need of them. They must take a lot of waking up, indeed. After Richmond I would make the long climb over the Pennines, and over the higher hills of the Lakes, before I would drop down to that other sea by another abbey another Irish saint had founded – she was born, according to her legend, quite soon after Oswy held his synod. Of all those earlier stages before Richmond little trace remains in memory; after, as sharp as a pin. Why the difference? Puzzling.

But Rievaulx, and the chains of thought to which it led, does come very clear: HD, one might say. I had a sort of expectation of it, for (as so often happens) I had read about it before going there, and that always means that someone else's eyes get in the way, at least to start with. This time it was Dorothy Wordsworth, whose *Grasmere Journal* had been bedside reading. It was, I recall, a perfect morning, and the ruins were only just opening, so everywhere was quiet. First impression was how different this tidy, pretty place was to what it looked like when Dorothy came in July 1802 with her brother:

'14 July we got into a post chaise and went to Thirsk to Breakfast. We were well treated but when the Landlady understood that we were going to *walk* off and leave our luggage behind she threw out some saucy words in our hearing ... Arrived very hungry at Ryvaulx. Nothing to eat at the Millers, as we expected but, at an exquisitely neat farmhouse we got some boiled milk and bread. This strengthened us, and I went down to look at the Ruins – thrushes were singing, cattle feeding among green grown hillocks about the Ruins. These hillocks were scattered over with *grovelets* of wild roses and other shrubs. And covered with wild flowers. I could have stayed in this solemn quiet spot till evening but William was waiting for me, so in a quarter of an hour I went away. ... [The Abbey] stands in a larger valley in a Brotherhood of valleys of different lengths and breadths all woody, and running up into the hills in all directions.'

(The Wordworths' little walk – Thirsk to Rievaulx, then to Helmsley – puts me to shame: 23 miles and bit more. Mind you, they must have been pretty fit, for there are regular accounts in Dorothy's *Grasmere Journal* of walks from Grasmere to Keswick to see Coleridge — a mere 12 miles, but done regularly.) Dorothy's hillocks, of course, were the ruins. Now excavated and labelled, then they were just the heaps of unsaleable rubble left when Henry's Commissioners had done their work. And those men were thorough. Oh yes, they were thorough. But ruins soon green over, and nature takes back what once we thought we had tamed. The dog roses full of July butterflies, and hawthorns with berries beginning their autumn blush, and sloe bushes Dorothy would have seen, are now tidied away for another more informative sort of beauty, and on first seeing Rievaulx I could not help thinking of the contrast with J. M. W. Turner's picture of a 'Romantick' Tintern Abbey, covered in ivy and with bushes growing out of the walls: a building conservator's nightmare. Rievaulx must have been like that. There was, of course, a recommended viewpoint from which the ruins would look suitably 'picturesque' — a term made fashionable, almost a craze, by William Gilpin's *Observations on the River Wye, and Several Parts of South Wales, etc. Relative Chiefly to Picturesque Beauty; made in the Summer of the Year 1770* — as if in a painting by, say, Claude le Lorrain. This was after all the age when 'romantick' ruins, and comfortably elegiac feelings, were sought out by people 'of Taste'. Thomas Dunscombe, the then owner, built the Terrace along the valley precisely for this purpose in 1758.

But my imagination goes further back, for there are other memories sounding here. Peel away the patina of time — in so far as mere reading allows you to. If you had come over the hill and looked down into this valley, or that of Fountains Abbey, or Bolton, or Tintern, or wherever, in their heyday, you would have seen the smoke from the glass making and the brewery, smelt the reek of the tannery, heard the clangour of iron on iron from the forges. It is a fact, now hard to keep in mind to qualify the now peaceful scene, where your imagination, if you let it, hears the music-over film and TV producers consider 'religious', that the great religious houses were major economic centres, major employers of lay labour, and great innovators – of their nature they could take the long view – in technology and industry. At its height Rievaulx had 140 monks and many more lay brothers. They mined the local iron ore, and by the Dissolution they owned iron forges at Laskill in Bilsdale and at the abbey itself. Early forges needed two hearths – a bloom hearth to smelt the iron from the ore, melting it into spongy lumps – blooms – and then a string hearth where the impurities were beaten out of the red hot blooms. The monks were great improvers: water wheels powered trip hammers for the string hearth, and they could make 16cwt of iron a week, which by mediaeval standards is a lot. All that used vast quantities of charcoal, which in turn meant the management and coppicing on a 20 year rotation of acre upon acre of woodland. They also turned a vast expanse of moorland into a sheep farm, and by the end of the 1200s the abbey owned 12,000 sheep. And that points up a delicious irony. The austere Cistercians – Rievaulx was a Cistercian house – went into the wilderness to be ascetic and poor and contemplative. But their Rule gave them a duty of scholarship, which means writing and copying. No paper then – not till the thirteenth century did Christendom make paper. So you wrote on sheepskin – parchment. And you had to grow your own sheep. Which means you need a tannery, and the complicated skills of parchment making. One sheepskin equals one folio. Writing quite small, you need about 500 sheep to copy a Bible. But all those sheep you grow in the wilderness give you lots and lots of wool, and meat, which, being prudent, you sell … and before you know where you are you are very rich indeed. And the monastery's community, monks, lay brothers, lay workers and their families spread themselves in charitable works and beautiful buildings, building bridges and whatever, and are busy, busy … What they were, what these monks did, lies far closer to the heart of what European history has been than many of those battles I now can't always remember between largely interchangeable princes. Any number of men clad in various fashions of ironmongery noisily knocking each other off horses are much less representative of what was really going on, what really mattered, of what we, late in time, have come to take for granted, than a man in a rough monk's habit patiently sharpening a quill and dipping it into the iron-gall ink he had made himself, while another supervises the building of a new and efficient mill or bloomery. The quiet mycelium of scholarship works underground. In time it fruits, surprising through the familiar earth.

I once spent some time in a monastery. It does not matter why, now, though that time to keep silence was important. But that short experience qualifies how I now can look at this tidy Heritage Site, and I can almost hear – just listen that bit more carefully – the voices, centuries of them, in the ancient daily Office. In 1132 12 monks from austere Clairvaux were sent to start up this new Abbey miles from anywhere in this almost empty land. In 1134, Ailred, born in Hexham, son of a priest, educated at Durham, Master of the Household at Roxburgh[10] of

[10] Roxburgh, at the strategic confluence of the Tweed and Teviot, was once a key town in southern Scotland, an important stronghold of the Gododdin, and a royal seat until the time of Robert the Bruce, who ordered its castle's destruction to deny its value to the English.

David I, King of Scotland, joined the quiet little community in its wooden buildings by the chattering river. Eight years later he had become its novice master, guiding and training postulants, a job requiring tact and understanding as well as firmness and authority. By 1147 he is Abbot, the community has now grown hugely to about 640 men – think of the logistics of that speed of growth! – and he begins the huge building project that made some of the buildings the beauty of whose ruins still can stir my heart. He also found time to write two books which are still read (I have well-thumbed second-hand copies myself: *The Mirror of Charity,* and *On Spiritual Friendship*). His saintliness meant that soon after he died in 1167 his relics were venerated: the east end of the church he built was rebuilt to house them. They were scattered to the four winds in the storm of 1538.

You know things, as facts, very often, and too often they may not register on the mind in any way that hits your emotions and alters the way you see. It is when facts do become inward that they hit you: the shock may take years, and wind you like a well-directed blow when it comes. The museum at Rievaulx – well, you've paid the entrance fee for the site and you might as well go round it. I know quite a bit – it's my job, after all – about the Dissolution of the Monasteries, but I don't think that I had fully hoisted in the details of what dissolving a house was actually like, nor the efficient effort that went into its destruction until I came to Rievaulx. That museum certainly landed an unexpected emotional punch on me. Perhaps seeing, literally *realising*, the cold administrative tidiness of it all, was why I remember Rievaulx so clearly, why ever since then I look at every similar site with the shock waves still resounding. When the deplorable Henry VIII's Commissioners came, they were businesslike, factual, with a job to do quite unemotionally, like any accountant or administrator: they noted that the Abbey consisted of 72 buildings, and recorded its exact possessions. They recorded the abbot, 21 monks, 102 lay brothers, and the Abbey's income of £351 a year. But their minutely detailed ledgers could not record the hymns of praise that sounded in the vaults of the choir or the dying of centuries of brothers in the infirmary. To be sure, the monks, now to be turned out into the world, would be given pensions, which (to the Crown's credit) were paid, as was standard procedure. But who were they without their community, their career, to put it no higher? The monastic buildings themselves were simply confiscated by the Crown, and often sold for a knockdown price by a cash-strapped Henry to the latest set of toadies or cronies. The commissioners set men – 'It ain't my fault, mate, it's just a job, innit?' – to work to strip anything of any even tiny value, not just the useful ashlar on the walls but also the very nails from the timbers of the roof, each painstakingly extracted with pincers for melting down. The wood was sold: I know one Elizabethan manor house near Cambridge where the roof is two hundred years older, recycled from a nearby dissolved Abbey. The lead of Rievaulx's roof was stripped, melted down into pigs, and one they left behind, because a now unstable wall fell on it, sits in the museum at Rievaulx, with the king's stamp of ownership on it. For some reason looking at that, a guiltless lump of lead, gave me a feeling of revulsion: St Augustine did remark that the only difference between a brigand and a monarch was that one was more successful than the other. And the same happened at all the other houses big and small – Jervaulx, Egglestone, Fountains, wide-spreading Whalley, little Marrick, Anglesey and Denny near this house, and so on. Henry granted the site of Rievaulx to Thomas Manners, one of his advisers – his second cousin, actually – whom he created Earl of Rutland. (Some) people did well out of/at the Reformation. More ruined choirs … In all the crises that turn lives and cultures upside down, there are the accountants, doing the quiet sums. In the Parker Library in Corpus Christi College, in Cambridge, the Librarian, Christopher de Hamel, once showed me a document which records what they paid for the faggots for burning Thomas Cranmer and what his last breakfast of a few figs and nuts cost. For your account does have to balance.

That was one of the things Rievaulx's ruins woke in my mind, suddenly focussing memories of other ruins like Melrose or Dryburgh, Jedburgh or Lanercost, Thetford or Bury, Furness or Shap, where for generations daily prayer, daily honouring of the things that are of God, had been offered. The human story … the thought kept – keeps – coming back: what must it have been like to live through such a tumultuous period, so sudden a storm? What must it have been like to be one of the ones who made it happen, when you have started something, possibly in good faith, you cannot then stop? Every fixed point, everything you had learned as a child to rely on, to trust, was being turned upside down; old wisdom, old custom, thrown out of the window and then the very window itself was destroyed by what many then called 'newefanglenessse'? Language itself is purged, and the thought police watch for any backsliding.[11] Heartbreak. And

---

[11]   I am not exaggerating: a statute of Henry VIII makes *thinking* treason a capital offence. It's dressed up in suitably dignified language, of course, but there was a fat chance of getting off if you were hauled up before one of his show trials. And execution for treason meant the Crown got your goods. It would.

yet we should know: we are living through just such a period. And so in the pretty, manicured ruins where families picnic and children play, I see a ghost of the pain and anguish that men and women suffered as all their anchors were cut away and the storms rose higher in the name (as always) of some bogus thing called 'Reform' or 'Progress' or the whole family of '-isms.' Such periods do come to an end, but rarely well.

Set into the wall above the door into what was the last Abbot's lodging, a carving has survived (perhaps by the same man who carved a similar one at ruined Fountains) which speaks of other imperatives, other values, other – well, challenges to comfortable norms. Gabriel, much weathered, kneels before Mary with his terrifying news of her high favour and his message of the ultimate powerlessness of earthly power:

> Angelus ad virginem,
> Subintrans in conclave,
> Virginis formidinem
> Demulcens, inquit 'Ave!' …

You can muse, pointlessly, too much: and cheerfulness does keep breaking in, as Oliver Edwards said to Dr Johnson. It was a magically beautiful morning, and I had very good sandwiches. *Deo gratias.*

Looking back, I think the thing that was most significant and enduringly memorable about the whole walk was the sense of walking back into a deep human past, a landscape with pressing, increasingly insistent, almost resonant memory, as the high hills drew closer – even when, as in the Lakes, it was a landscape that over decades had been utterly familiar to me and my family. If you like, walking over the ridge where on the one side the rivers flow to the North Sea and on the other to the Irish was more than just a literal watershed: it was a change of key in how one could think. Familiar became unfamiliar: even the lovely landscape of the Lakes I had known so well and for so long was coming into focus as a palimpsest scribbled over by many, many hands, people who loved it, worked it, thought they owned it. When Constable painted Derwentwater there were hardly any trees: they had all been cut for charcoal for the ore smelting. What the paintings and photos now show as 'unspoiled', 'natural' beauty is actually post-industrial. The placenames recall forgotten Norsemen, or what they called a hill or a crag, and some of the rivers speak of an even more ancient people speaking an ancestor of Welsh. Some of Swaledale's or Craven's field boundaries go back to the Neolithic: once you have a drystone wall in place, why bother to move it? It's an awful lot of heavy work, and if it falls over, well, you have the stone ready to hand to build it up again. If you know where and how to look you can see where the old, forgotten people honoured their dead. Indiscriminately, patient lichens, grey, green, old gold, spread, slow but slow, over the cherub's face on a grandiose eighteenth-century tombstone in a graveyard and the weathered stone bones of what was a kist burial or a barrow. They slowly eat stone into soil.

I set off one early morning, west, out of Richmond, into light rain. No matter: a journey to be done.

+ + +

The small rain eased and the sun came out. Going up the dale through the sweet smell of the recently cut hayfields, with the

Pennine moors before me, I discovered just how many different sorts of stone stiles there might be. There were no two alike, and none easy in the damp with a big rucksack. Below Gunnerside I encountered what can only be called Fat Man's Agony, two vertically set slabs of stone closing in a V to a tiny boot-wide gap at the bottom. I admired the economic plotting of the land by field walls straddled by little gray stone hay barns, each with a foot in two fields for ease of feeding the animals. Each sat where the walls climbed a low river terrace, and the hay could be loaded from the higher ground and then taken out from the lower: the old folk knew about saving work.

Curiosity sometimes wins over sober practicality and sense. I had a fixed time to do the walk, and strictly I ought to have kept to my planned route. But Gunnerside – well, the name itself was attraction enough: once, a man called Gunnar had a summer pasture, a *saetr,* here. He probably lived about the same time as Kraki. The women and children would have come up with the cattle from the main farm for the months when the men would stay behind to do the haymaking and the harvest. The summer grass would have given good milk to be made into butter and cheese for the winter. The name Gunnar had a special resonance too: just before Norse Gunnar named this farm – God knows who had it before him – his namesake Gunnar Hamundarson in Iceland followed his tragic destiny: the name resonated with all the pity and sorrow that had so moved me when I read the *Saga of Burnt Njal.* But, more practically: this green and pleasant valley, which looks as if it has not changed much since Gunnar came in the tenth century or so, was not so long ago part of the industrial heart of England, thick with smoke from the smelting and the charcoal burning. Lead: lots and lots of it. At the top

of Gunnerside Ghyll is one of the richest veins in this part of
the country, Blakethwaite, and it kept men in work for several
generations. And slowly poisoned them too. The pretty cottages
of the village housed the miners, many of them affected by lead:
high blood pressure, pain in joint and muscle, failing memory
or concentration, headache ... infertility. On an impulse I
decided from the direct way to turn my steps and walk up the
ghyll to the moor. The path was steep enough: imagine doing
this every day in all weathers to get to work! It begins to ease
as you come out of the young trees – all the old woodland was
cut for charcoal – into a desolation of stones. Just a bit further,
and to the west the huge scar of Gunnerside North Hush, to
the east, Bunton, Friarfold, and Gorton Hushes. Consider: the
vein is near the surface, and you want to get as much ore out as
quickly as you can. Profit rules. Adits are slow to make, and in
them you can only work the small face at the end of each branch
of the tunnel. But if your rich vein happens to be in a ghyll near
a stream you can do it much more quickly. Dam the stream,
make a temporary lake, and then break the dam: the noise gives
the name, recorded first in 1750 by the *OED*. Sure, the rush of
water is destructive of much downstream, but it most efficiently
strips away the overburden, and you can pick up the ore in plain
daylight. And you can do it again, and again. So the little sykes,
coming off the moor to join the beck, are dammed, and when
you have done it once and cleared up the pickings, you do it yet
again. In a blink of an eye more was carved out of the hillside
than the beck would have done in a thousand years. It was a dirty
trade. On the moor, higher up, you can see the long masonry
flues that carried some of the gases and smoke from the smelting
of the ore, and all around is dead soil: nothing will grow for

many years. Bits of the ore still lie around: somewhere I think I have the bit of galena I picked up. It is probably with all the other stones and bits of rock, the plethora of paperweights, that I have picked up over the years: 'specimens' was what I called them, each tagged the memory of where a younger me found it, and they will mean nothing to those who clear up this house when I am gone.

The scars of this wasteland will heal, slowly. It may take a few centuries, but the world has time. Meanwhile, you have to admire the ingenuity, and perhaps regret the values behind it. Save for scale, there is not much to choose between this wrecking of a landscape and the felling of the rainforests. 'We need jobs ...' 'We need to make a profit.' Nothing changes. Will we ever learn?

Returning, sweaty, sobered and thoughtful, I followed the river to a field at Keld, where a cheerful farmer told me I could camp in his field, 'and welcome, and don't ye mind them bullocks.' (I didn't – and don't – but they do make a noise when they tear at the grass outside the tent.) Next day, the Swale gradually got smaller and more juvenile, playful even, as I followed it upstream. I admired the low steady bright curve of its peat-brown fall where it went over the millstone grit sills. Gradually the path climbed up, with the river as company, into the higher hills, to a treeless moor where the stream gave up. The wide expanse of boggy ground, rough tussocky *molinia* grassland with rushes in the wetter patches, was dotted with grouse butts and an occasional field shelter for the August guns as they took their lunch. Bits of drier ground were purpling with heather. Larksong gave way to the spine-tingling, bubbling calls of curlews. The occasional grouse exploded from a sitting start into fast flight in that disconcerting way they have, shouting at me, 'Go back! Go back!' But despite the sun warm on my back, the clouds ahead were massing, and I crossed the Pennine watershed by Nine Standards Rigg on Hartley Fell, in what had in minutes turned from intermittent sunlight to suddenly angry wind and horizontal rain, and I sploshed my way between already sodden peat hags. To pause on the summit and look at the collection of nine drystone cairns (which can be seen for miles when it is not raining) was a wet step too far, to my shame, and I pressed on down and rejoined the old road to the packhorse bridge over the Eden.

Nowadays, there is always for me a sense of let down when you approach a town or village of which you know, but do not yet know, through a litter of ribbon development and garages and bungalows. But Kirkby Stephen from this route is different, much more like approaching a town centuries ago must have been. I joined a route, part of an old packhorse route over the Pennines, that dropped down steeply from the moor into lush fields walled in drystone, then fringed by tall trees. Soon the chatter of a beck that ran into the Eden was drowned in the deeper note of the rain-swelling Eden itself where it passes over a lip of the hard Brockram limestone. A mothers' meeting of supercilious ewes with rain-beaded, wet coats stood on my path: as I neared they grudgingly moved aside, and then decided they would, after all, run as if in panic, and then after fifty yards, all stopped and stared. I dropped down through their meadow which cascades steeply down the slope to the humpback bridge. The parapets were made low enough to allow the load on the horses' pack saddles to clear them – the ideal height on which to rest your backpack. It is narrow, and you cannot get past a person crossing the other way. Below, in an eddy of the swirling current, two mallards and a duck dabbled for the free food the spate was bringing down. And then you are right in the middle of the town, tarmac underfoot. A good way to arrive.

I found a respite that night in a Homely House at Kirkby Stephen, where a kind lady, who over later years became a friend, dried out my socks. Next morning she gave me a magnificent breakfast and while I ate it talked of her love for church music. (And gave me an Everyman copy her father had owned of Jacob Boehme's *The Signature of All Things, with Other Writings,* which, though I dipped into it and liked what I saw, is still on the pile of 'To Be Read Properly One Day' books.) And then, replete and later than I had intended because we had had a lot to talk about, on a day that seemed (but wasn't) too bright to last, I was off again. I popped into the church, for curiosity – again! – made me go and look at the Loki Stone, an eighth-century carving of Loki, most treacherous of the Norse gods, bound and chained. Nobody knows where it was originally or what it was: for years it was lying in a dump of old tombstones outside the east end – yet it is one of only two carvings like this in Europe. Once again, you stub your toes on what was Today for unknowable people in an unknowable world long ago. The Harcla and Musgrave tombs in the church remind of old power and influence – and they reminded me of the tragic Pilgrimage of Grace in 1537 when so many of the northern commons and small gentry from round here rose up against the tyranny of Thomas Cromwell, Henry VIII's creature, and his destruction of all they had ever known and loved in their church. It failed, of course, and reprisals were cruel. One Thomas Musgrave – there are still Musgraves in the area – was one of the local leaders, and on two occasions took refuge in the tower of this church to escape capture, and worse, by the vengeful Duke of Norfolk – Bluff King Hal had ordered hanging, drawing and quartering. The Pilgrimage had been peaceful, loyal to the Crown, disciplined: its banner was the Five Wounds of the Crucified Lord.

Sometimes your historian's knowledge of what happened, which your mind can usually keep fairly safely objective and analytic, turns round and clobbers you. I found myself suddenly on my knees, praying incoherently for pardon for the cruelties we visit on each other. (Funny, how that impulse suddenly came.) Then, get on: late already. I walked fast past the cattle market, loud with pens of sheep and protesting bullocks, to find the path out of the town that would lead me to the old, old tracks across the limestone. It got lonelier: after the farm, clearly not many people had trodden this way recently. The path climbed up through the fields to the Iron Age settlement at Waitby, marked only by humps and bumps in grass and clumps of nettles. There were buxom mushrooms whitely punching up through the turf. I'd like to think the nettles went back to the time when humankind, a phosphate-concentrating species, enriched that soil with their refuse and more intimate things, but a derelict galvanised feeding trough suggested that it was simply where the sheep had been fed for years. Sheep nibbled delicately as their smaller ancestors had done thirty centuries ago, when the people who built the square fields and the round huts had found this land good, and between their settlements had made these very tracks, some walled for droving stock, by which I walked. I saw no-one. Curlews, the bird *par excellence* of this high open land, called. There are far fewer than there used to be. Once this airy landscape was busy with work and the noise of animals and people, and sometimes, when I have walked here in fair winter weather, I have fancied I heard their voices speaking when the wind combed the brown bents of the tired grasses. For the past is always present. And what was it you glimpse out of the tail of your eye, or was it just watering in the wind?

Perhaps. Certainly unknowable, for if it were knowable, demonstrable, categorizable, it would be in our world, on our wavelength – literally. But just as on the Helm, one senses – well … Someone – I cannot remember who – once told me something said by the Rev. Jim Bear Jacobs, a Mohican pastor in the Church of All Nations, which was so electrifying I noted it down: 'You Europeans think of events occurring on a timeline. An event distant in time is distant from you. But we indigenous peoples think of events as occurring in a place. Whenever we are near that place, we are near that event, no matter when it happened. For us places hold stories, and become sacred because of the stories they hold.'

+ + +

The path had now opened out into what some might have thought a long narrow field, but I recognised this as yet one more of those places where herds of slowly moving cattle and sheep had been stopped to feed and to rest on their long, slow journey to their market – in Scotland they called them 'trysts'. Five to ten miles a day the slow herds would travel … For cattle droving covered these islands with a network of routes now forgotten, all bringing the cattle and sheep from the furthest lonely farm to gather at the great markets, and they had to have places to pause, to water, to feed, on the way. Thence, I dropped down steeply to

the busy beck at Smardale Bridge on its noisy hurry to join the
Eden, past the pillow mounds which showed where once upon
a time someone who held the Lordship of the Manor – probably
the Gilbertine canons of Ravenstonedale Priory who had been
given the manor, I think, by Torphin fitz Robert (what was his
story?) all those years back – had made the artificial burrows
for the delicate rabbits the Normans had introduced into the
England they had made their own. (The rabbits soon became
very able to fend for themselves, but for centuries their fur and
their flesh remained jealously guarded, the one fashionable, the
other a delicacy.)

I paused at that loveliest of remote bridges. At one end of
its humpback, broad as it had to be for driven cattle, a headlong
little beck crosses the path in wet weather, and where the water
gathers ages ago people paved it with great slabs of gritstone.
They are worn dished by centuries of feet and hooves. Here,
I had to leave the old route, cut deep into the landscape and
this slope, and strike off to the right: another climb, up through
the low banks of the Iron Age/Romano-British settlement of
Severals, and the way goes on, and on, over the high limestone,
where sometimes the ancient bones of the land break through
the thin flesh of soil. Rain, slightly acid, melts limestone away
in time, and in the dark deep clefts so left along the lines of
weakness, where the assiduous nibbling of sheep cannot reach,
grow little hawthorns, and the shiny green of hart's tongue fern.
My father grew those in pots, for reasons I never understood.
But he liked them.

The path, easy enough going, suddenly dropped down the
steep side of the Potts valley. I forded the stream by the deserted
farm. It's an obvious place to put a farm: here the valley bottom

opens out a bit, the old trackway crosses there, and you are low enough down the river to ensure that even in the driest years it will have water. Higher up, its flow depends on how much water is held in the limestone. Once – not long ago, in fact –this farm was a lovely house loud with the noise of people and children and cattle and dogs – the noises the forgotten folk who made the square fields and built the burial cairns and barrows would have known – but the farm was not paying, and it was quite a way to get to the main road, and now the well-set stone house year by year sinks into ruin as the ivy grasps it in its soft grey fingers. Only the stream and the odd sheep hear the noise when a bit more of the roof falls in. Yesterday's rain had made the river in spate, and all the little seasonal springs, excitedly bubbling up from the limestone, were spouting like fountains into their channels, long dry enough for grass to grow in their beds.

I saw nobody in all this long stretch, and one could almost believe in a quieter, emptier England, the sort of England I can just remember, where a man's pace measured the times of miles, as since time beyond memory. Till now – yet in the first weeks of the lockdown after COVID struck, for a while I could not think why the light was different, the world was quiet, the air smelt different, and then realised that was how the world was when I was young, before the ambient pollution we take for granted did its work. But there is no going back: after a few hours the world I had left for a spell reminded me of itself. Three miles east of the M6 I smelt it on the bright wind. Two miles east I heard its imperious rumble. I crossed it on the bridge, and dropped into Shap, where the land changes dramatically along a fault from porous limestone to hard volcanic and metamorphic rock. In a wet season black mud lurks for the feet of the unwary. Cross the road by the ruins of Shap Abbey and the range of flowers and plants changes almost as sharply; you see the fault, underlined by the rush of the noisy river Lowther that hurries along it. That night I treated myself to a meal in the pub, could not find a quiet place to pitch the little tent – that is the trouble with villages – and so spent a night in the cells. The B&B had been the old police station, and a night behind the big, studded door with its barred window could certainly have been much worse, with bacon and black pudding and two eggs and sausage and tomatoes and mushrooms with toast and coffee for breakfast. But somehow I don't think ancient malefactors got that.

But let that be: on with the rucksack and off to where the high hills closed the west. I dropped down to the Lowther by the Abbey ruins, and paused for a moment to contemplate vicissitude, the temporariness of the things we call permanent. My trouble is that intellectually I can accept that cycle with a certain equanimity, even smugness – Princes, Presidents, Prime Ministers, dictators all pay the debt of humanity – but faced with the evidence of a real story with real people in it, even if I do not know them, I cannot help but imagine their pain. It all seemed so secure ... This community, never large, of the austere Premonstratensians, had been around here since the 1190s, slowly becoming wealthy through wool, recycling much of that wealth into supporting the poor, maintaining roads and bridges, into education and hospitals, and in the building boom of the fifteenth century spent a huge sum to the Glory of God on a new tower in the latest fashion. Two generations later, their world turned upside down. Just as the kindly and fertile limestone can here switch in a few short yards to the dour sourness of the harder rocks, so suddenly can the world change.

The track I had chosen took me up Swindale, a valley I had never travelled before. It's a bit off the beaten track, and I like that. It is a fair pull up to the head of the valley at Swindale Head, and then a still stiffer pull up to the ridge, and then down into Mardale, where one of thirsty Manchester's reservoirs now covers the old village. In really dry weather the old village, or what is left of it, rises from its grave. I was on the old Corpse Road. Freshets of water were running down its incised steepness, ponding behind rocks, picking at the stones, and occasionally, as I watched while getting my breath, carrying off a pebble. Once upon a time, when parishes were bigger, settlements smaller and houses far asunder, burial in consecrated ground often meant carrying the dead over roads like this, over miles of wilderness, up hill and down dale, to the parish church. Mardale as a chapelry of Shap had no right of burial till the 1740s. The dead of that little hamlet, strapped in their woollen shrouds to the back of a pony, were carried miles over the hills to the parish church in Shap. Roads like these litter the west and north of these islands, largely forgotten. They are on Skye, and Lewis, and the Lakes, and Wales. There are some forgotten under tarmac, remembered only in a garbled name: The Causeway in the next Fenland village to me is not that at all, but the Corpse Way from the outlying hamlet to the parish Church. I have followed another corpse road near Grasmere, where is a flat stone, the Resting Stone: here the late lamented was put down as the bearers got their breath back for the next pull up the slope. No problem going down: this was a one-way traffic. Now walkers in bright clothes eat their sandwiches on it.

At Mardale Head I had a decent break, and almost fell asleep in the fitful sun. But: get on, hoist on the pack, and then the path took me steeply up Nan Bield Pass. Once it was a major route, with along it the ruins of little stone shelters ('bield' means 'shelter') for travellers benighted or caught out by the westerly storms which can swirl wickedly down this steep glacier-plucked side of the fell. Then I followed the ridge over Mardale Ill Bell to High Street, where on long gone summer days they used to hold horse races. From it, you can get a grand view when it is clear (it wasn't) to the ridge of which Helvellyn is the peak. The last time I was up here was in a late spring snowstorm, in almost a whiteout, carefully making my way from cairn to cairn, constantly checking the compass. Now a pipit is singing, and on the way up I saw a wheatear and heard a stonechat. But I can see there is dirty weather coming in from the west, and the first spots of rain greeted me on the top, just as I reached the Roman road. For the Romans built a major road across this top – you can still easily make it out – to connect their forts at Ambleside and Brougham, and you can't help wondering about the complex equations of a much, much smaller population, the huge amount of labour needed, and the logistics of feeding and clothing them. And no earthmoving machines, just muscle and not even spades of steel.

Then the rain came on, heavy and determined. As I was dropping down the steep slope into Hayeswater Gill from the Roman road, it was unkindly: it blew inside my hood on the wind blowing up the valley. I stopped thinking about the Romans. Tiny globes of water on the leaves of mountain lady's bedstraw wobbled as fresh drops hit the plant, and the crag behind me was intermittently draped in a muslin of rain. Dripping, I squelched along the path into Patterdale, and found food and beer at the pub. This was a night, I decided as I steamed, for not even trying to camp. (Our forebears might not have had that choice.) Yet before I turned in the rain had passed and a magnificence of stars chided me for being a wimp: why electric light when you have got us, sending you our light from aeons ago?

Next day dawned bright and sharp, everything washed and clean after the deluge of the evening before. The sun was warm on my back as I tramped up Grisedale, knees brushing the sparkling drops off the wet grasses overhanging the narrow path that the passage of feet had trod. Then over the col and down to Dunmail Raise. The holiday traffic paused me at the side of the road, waiting, waiting to cross as the cars cleared their throats with a change of gears as the ascent eased. Full-bellied clouds were gathering, though, as thermals pushed up the damp air through the dewpoint, and soon another band of rain caught me for the crossing of the next ridge from Wythburn. At last I descended from the morass of High Tove, a peaty sponge pretending to be a hill, about which it is difficult to find anything affectionate to say – not even the estimable Alfred Wainwright can. It is especially nasty after heavy rain. There had been heavy rain. I dropped down the neatly planned zigzags of the old path, into Watendlath, which Hugh Walpole in his *Herries Chronicles* made Judith Paris' home. The National Trust, who own the farm, have put a neat slate plate on the wall to mark that, for people make a real pilgrimage – the Herries Trail – to this site of a fiction, just as they gather outside 'Juliet's Balcony' and take photographs in Verona. Then, leaving one of the loveliest of tarns behind – the trout were rising well – over the low pass into beloved, familiar Borrowdale, dropping down from the pass into so many memories of walking there over the years with loved ones, some now gone ahead on the journey, and memories of others' stories told of their own memories. Memories too, of the first grandchild discovering a beck for the first delighted time, and beginning to fill up his sensibility. A palimpsest of memory, an endless perspective down the arches of the years, which will not end with me.

It was now a beauteous evening, calm and free,

> The holy time is quiet as a Nun
> Breathless with adoration; the broad sun
> Is sinking down in its tranquillity;

Wordsworth gets it right so often. In the low sun from the west the late rain shone prismatically on the leaves, and the beck sang a loud deep song over the stones by the village. Fat Herdwick gimmers – in their woolly jumpers they care not about rain – contentedly grazed on the flat in-bye land in the valley bottom. A sign by the National Trust loos advertised sheep dog trials, and cream teas at the farm cafe. Too late for both ...

I thought the brightness of the evening would not last long. The moon's parselenion as I walked back from the pub that evening was warning enough. The morrow indeed brought cloud, and mist wreathing the tops. Yet another front was on its way. Never mind, press on: pack up the tent while it is still more or less dry, and get moving. At Seathwaite I started the ascent to Sty Head Pass, carefully ignoring (where I could) the straight-up-the-hill scars made by impatient modern walkers in heavy boots so that I could follow what was left of the delectably graded, paved zig zags the old folk made for their strings of pack horses going over the pass to Wasdale and down to the port which the Romans improved at Ravenglass.

How old? Who knows? These passes and paths have been used since men came to this land. The Romans made their fort, Mediobogdum, on Hardknott Pass to guard their traffic to their important harbour at Ravenglass – perhaps that fort was one of the most draughty postings in the whole empire. Much later, a lot of the stone walls on the hills were put up by the Cistercians of Furness Abbey, tending the sheep that made them so rich; some walls, the wiggly ones, are much, much older than the mere twelfth century. I took a break by the tarn at Sty Head, a place full of memories going back to before I was a father. Once, when I was an undergraduate, young and foolish (not all are), on a winter walking and reading party with the Dean of my College, I set off across its snow-covered ice and fell in, and was sternly sent, wetly, back to Rosthwaite and a bath, with the Dean's understated reproach of 'Impetuous youth!' ringing in my ears. There was once, a good deal later, a languorous day in dappling sunlight with the children and our first Labrador splashing in the shallows while we dozed after a lunch of pork pies. But no dozing today, for a mean little wind chivvied me to get a bit of mileage behind me before the rain came. Over the higher pass of Windy Gap, which lived up to its name, then down the Tongue to Black Sail hostel, and the long walk down Ennerdale. I was still miraculously dry. The rain arrived just as I settled down for the night in a caravan at the foot of the lake on a farm where a cheerful lady offers Bed and Breakfast. The accelerating pattering on the caravan roof was even, well, pleasant. And less noisy than rain on the tent.

But this rain really meant it. It was coming down in stair rods by morning, and gusty with a westerly behind it. The lady arrived at the caravan with my breakfast on a tray covered with a plastic sheet in the dimples of which puddles were forming. The food was good, and properly substantial, if somewhat cool. The weather was filthy, and this ought to have been a staying in and reading day. But I was a day behind schedule and really needed to catch that train at St Bees, for work, however remote it felt, would not wait, and curiously beside the point getting back to it seemed after the imperatives of these last days.

I'd never really thought about St Bees much – it was just a place with a big headland sticking out into the Irish Sea, and the place Wainwright chose as the starting point for his Cross Country Walk – which he did in the opposite direction to the one I took. Yet here I was, tramping towards it as the goal of this long walk, where I could catch a train to take me back to work and 'normality': but was it quite the same person going back? What does this walk add up to? As the miles pass, your – well, my – mind often goes into idling, associative, mode as the rhythm of long walking quietens the itch to connected, purposeful thought – but, far worse, the mind can get stuck on the awful treadmill of those thoughts that go nowhere except pain, or resentment, or feeling hard done by, which sometimes won't go away and seem to fit the rhythm of your tread. I made myself think – as one does, or as oddballs like me do – about the people long ago who made and walked the lanes and paths I was treading. Someone planned their gradients, the way they zig zag economically up and over the hills, organised their paving – a huge job – of which you can still occasionally see traces. But such work implies a complex social structure, division of labour, and some sort of coordinating authority. Politics, in other words. Some gratitude to the Old Ones is called for.

So often we are still living on the capital our forebears left us, and we take it for granted. They set the unnoticed coordinates of our lives far more often than we think. What is it Tennyson says in 'Locksley Hall'? 'I am the heir of all the ages.' Yes: and the legacy is curse as well as blessing. Much to say about that ... not now. Then came to my mind thoughts of those of all sorts and conditions of men who, centuries before me, had walked this route to St Bees, walking it as a spiritual exercise, as pilgrims (before the Royal Injunctions of the tyrant Henry VIII banned pilgrimage). What was in their mind as they made their way to the ancient shrine of St Bega? I tried to imagine, as the road got harder and the rain wetter, what I would have been wearing: a wide brimmed felt hat or a hood, a long grey cloak, boots that had only soft leather soles – most mediaeval folk of humble station must have had permanently wet and cold feet. I would have carried a staff – as I do, but never need to use it as my forebears would have done to fend off troublesome dogs. If I did pilgrimages often – some did and the name Palmer is a fossil of that – I might well have worn little lead badges, souvenirs of various holy shrines visited – the sort of things people regularly fish out of the mud of the Thames – much as people now stick labels on the windows of their cars saying 'Torquay', or 'We've Been To [fill in as required]'.

I was getting, and feeling, wetter with the warm rain driving once more into the hood of my anorak and running down my chest. I could not help thinking of how heavy those long wool cloaks would become as they soaked, of the drip from the soaked felt hat, and how long they would take to dry. And how foul the ways would be in the acted-out metaphor of the Christian life, the penance of travel to an end of – Welcome? Healing? (Bunyan, in clayey Bedfordshire, gives us a pretty good idea of what the real, not just metaphorical, sloughs could be like.) What was I, indeed, complaining about? The old ones would have given so much for the lightness of Gore-Tex – so do I, actually, for my first clothing specifically for walking on the hills was a heavy canvas smock and hobnailed boots. When wet that smock would stand up on its own for days. The boots made sparks on the road on a dark, dry night. (I do quite miss that.)

I read up about St Bega later, when the slow leaven of having walked a pilgrim route without committing yet to being a pilgrim began to work in the mind. (You can't be too careful about what you let in.) She was, her legend says, an Irish princess – there was apparently quite a supply of them – who to avoid enforced marriage (of course) to some Norse notable escaped alone across the Irish Sea to this spot that bears her name. It is a nice story, not wholly implausible after 850 or so when Norsemen, notable or not, came in on almost every tide in this part of the world. Carved stones in the Priory church in St Bees, which was controlled (like Kirkby Stephen) by the Benedictine house of St Margaret at York – gosh, the Benedictine monks might have travelled by the very route I took! – give clear evidence that Irish-Norse Vikings settled here in the tenth century, about the time Bega is supposed to have lived. Until the calamitous 1530s, the monks at the Priory were guardians of a Ring which they claimed had been hers. People still swore oaths on it in legal processes – exactly as the Norsemen swore oaths and ratified treaties on a Ring of Power, exactly as Guthrum did when he made peace with Alfred in 878, and the Icelandic sagas have many instances of swearing by special rings kept in special places. But ... in Old

English *beag* means 'bracelet' or 'arm ring' – indeed the sort of thing on which one might, if so disposed, swear. It is possible the corruption of the word, swapping the 'a' and 'g' round and making a personal name, might have led to growth of a story and a legend of a saintly owner. But if enough people believe it, and make their pilgrimage to the shrine and pay their sincere devotions … the place remembers that devotion as real enough, and the richness of the building is evidence of it. After all, so I have come to think, the historical actuality of a sacred site – one could name so many – or the genuineness of the relics they hold or held, is not always the most important thing about it, for pilgrim sites – like the relics they once held – speak to an older variety of truth.

It was the Normans, latecomers up here (and they did not find the locals easy), who built the fine red building the truncated remains of which outface the worst the west wind can throw at it. But the years of struggle show on that soft red stone. The priory was set up a few years before Ailred founded Rievaulx in that remarkable twelfth century. William le Meschin, ('the Younger', not *le méchant*) Lord of Egremont, who had been on the First Crusade that established the Frankish kingdoms in Palestine in 1099, gave the land and founded a Benedictine house for a prior and six monks (and their lay brothers) on the site of an existing church. It was an act of piety: the cynical might say he was trying to buy his way out of trouble with the Almighty for what he had done on that expedition to bash the Saracens, but I think and trust that people's motives are often far more mixed and generous than we think. (All those mediaeval pilgrims of all stations, including the humblest, braving the hardships of those journeys, dangerous by sea or land, of the great pilgrimages to Rome, to Jerusalem, to Santiago – can I really believe there was no genuine devotion in them, whatever mischief and shenanigans they got up to along the way? Flatly, no.)

As I came out of the shelter of the headland, and saw the Priory, the wind hit me, fierce and overmastering as it came off the grey-white sea, and the hard rain stung my face. It was a relief to come in at last out of this storm, to pass under the carved archivolts, deeply weathered, of the Norman doorway, to come in out of the dull roar of the stormy sea into the cool quiet of the nave, a ship which was weathering the storm. I stood for a moment, and little pools of water formed round each boot. I dropped my rucksack, eased my shoulders from the pull of the straps. As there was nobody there except the angels, I stripped off to my wet underwear, put on less damp clothes. And sat, while the storm outside buffeted the old stones, erasing grain by grain yet more of the work of men's hands. How long I sat there I am not quite sure. I was not conscious of actually praying, or meditating – after all, that was not my habit: just of being inside, in shelter, quiet, stilled. But then I half-heard Time's winged chariot hurrying near, I stirred, and looked to where a rumour of the returning sun shone through the three lancet windows in the west.

I went outside, as the clouds broke, into a washed, bright world. On a stone lintel, a shaft of sunlight bathed in ephemeral glory St Michael locked in unending fight with the Dragon, as the twelfth-century carver had made him. I was in good time for the train to take me back to another reality.

But I was left with restlessness, and that will not now ever go away. Another journey. But whither, and why? And why not stop doing it with a certain reserve, caution about committing oneself, but plunge in at the deep end and do it properly? Take the risk: there are no guarantees. To set out on a pilgrimage is to throw down a challenge to everyday life. You do not know who will pick up your gauntlet.

4

DURABLE FIRE

'As you came from the holy land
Of Walsinghame,
Met you not with my true love
By the way as you came?' ...
(sometimes attributed, perhaps implausibly,
to Sir Walter Ralegh)

In the wracks of Walsingham
Whom should I choose
But the Queen of Walsingham
To be my guide and muse?
(Anonymous lament for Walsingham, ca. 1600)

What was it the Lady Richeldis, wife of Sir Geoffrey de Faverches, saw that strange day when the visions came? Were they holy or were they delusions? Why did Blessed Mary tell Richeldis (so she said) to build a replica of the Holy House of Nazareth in deepest Norfolk? Was the place *already* holy in some way? Who can know? But Richeldis did build it. Whatever it was, something happened. And people, no less sceptical, worldly, surly and curmudgeonly then than we are now, came to believe that something miraculous really had happened, that Walsingham *was* a special place, where worlds – or, if you prefer, different modes of being – intersect. That so many people for so long went in good faith to Walsingham *made* it holy: a place to which the way has been worn by countless feet, in some places literally. Sometimes, indeed, they walked the last flinty mile barefoot, removing their footwear at the Slipper Chapel: as Henry VIII did once before things went awry. In some stretches the old way has cut several feet deep into the soft landscape, and the land is marked by, perhaps remembers, the trudgers and riders in storm and shine, the tale-tellers, the jokers, the wide boys looking for mugs, the penitents, the holy-daymakers. Perhaps the pilgrim songs they all sang together to make the long miles seem shorter have not quite died away. The tramp of those feet sometimes, when you walk that way, seems to fall into step with yours. It is all mere imagination, auto-suggestion, of course. That half-heard jingle of harness behind me was of course only a bicycle bell. I think. But I can't forget one Evensong in the mediaeval church where my mother worshipped in her last years. While we in the front pew were singing the Magnificat I had this sudden *knowledge* that if I turned round I would see the church full of ancient faces.

So here I was, taking, self-consciously, almost self-ironically, the plunge: pilgrimage, explicitly that. Breaking cover at last. The hounds were giving tongue. It was a strange moment, putting on my boots at the back door of the familiar house explicitly for that purpose: this was a devotional pilgrimage, not just a long walk. So often those worn old friends have been called on for heavy duty in far places, in the Alps, the Lakes, Scotland, Iceland, Norway, and rarely for this soft countryside where gumboots are more my style. But this was different. I thought of those people centuries ago who would have sat at the door of their houses and laced on their boots: they knew that some of them on those hazardous journeys, their acted-out metaphor of the journey from birth to death, might never return, and if they did would not return unchanged. What that change might be – well, nothing is inevitable or predictable, of course: your body may make the journey, but it is what you carry inside, and burdens you can leave on the way, that makes it worth your while. Or not. Pilgrimage may be the only journey where you want to get rid of what you carry.

Worth trying – giving it a go, as the young might say. Don't expect anything.

The first misty dawn of September: dead still, silent save for the talkative woodpigeons in the ash tree I planted years ago, who can never shut up: 'My *toe* hurts, Betty …' and another replies, 'You're *so, so* stupid'. Dew on the grass, so that my boots are black with water in the first steps, and kick up an arc of droplets with each stride. You can see my prints where I have walked across the Green. The first chill of Autumn too: I am glad of my light coat, after weeks of walking in shirt sleeves. Today's is an easy stage, just some sixteen or so miles, and it will be dull, at least in the middle bits, with rather too much road, with no chance of getting off onto field paths. I know this bit of country very well too, though some bits I have not visited for years.

It's very hard not to go into my default attitudes: keep up a good pace, keep alert for all things great and small, even bright and beautiful, look critically at buildings that are worth attention and deduce their architectural history, perhaps indulge the sin of Envy when passing a Queen Anne house, or even a run of the mill Georgian. (I have never been keen on thatch and half timbering: poky and dark, all too often, and little head room. Nice from the outside.) Had I a companion, we would feel it necessary to make intelligent and improving conversation. But this time I don't. I am on my own.

I followed the edge of the Fen where it abuts what we in these parts call the high land, to the mystification of those who expect hills. It is an old clay track much cut up by winter tractors into hard late summer ruts. This was the old road, running round the spring line Fen from settlement to settlement, a thirsty man's route in this dry country. How old? God knows: flint scatters suggest at least Neolithic. The path then ran through fields of whispering stands of maize, a crop that never used to be grown here. The maize is higher than my head, and its tassels catch the sighs of a little breeze. Nothing grows beneath it. At the field edge, round my feet, catching at my trousers, are swags of later summer nettles and effete thistles, lolling over with the weight of dew and downy seed head. Inside a thicket of blackthorn and brambles by the young stream I glimpse a little clearing, where someone has put up a small, battered tent. The bushes arch over it. Nobody has been there for some time: the wall of nettles is too tall. There are beer cans lying where they were thrown. There is mould on the green flysheet of the tent, and a frying pan upside down inside: I can see in because the door is unzipped and tied back. There are dry leaves inside where they have blown. A puzzle, a reminder of the secrecy of even this most well-known countryside. It tells me nothing except that surprises are to be expected.

Then, following the stream, to the makeshift little bridge half covered by brambles – two planks and a scaffolding pole as handrail. Not many people come this way nowadays – far different from the times when this path I follow would have been a main way to the church from the hamlet by the Devil's Dyke. Crossing – and here I am where the moat would have ended – I skirt where the castle would have stood if King Stephen had ever finished it: the need for it disappeared when Geoffrey de Mandeville, a troublesome if able fellow, was killed there fighting against the king's forces. But Stephen did get as far as doing the earthworks and tipping the spoil all over the peasants' tofts. They cannot have been delighted. For

> I see nothing quite conclusive in the art of temporal
>   government
> But violence, duplicity and frequent malversation.
> King rules or barons rule:
> The strong man strongly and the weak man by caprice.

A couple of Sunday morning dogs bound up to me, tails wagging, tongues lolling: I like dogs, if not always their owners. I do have my usual supply of dog biscuits and they get a half each. Alms … A thousand years before Stephen started on the castle the Romans had a villa here, below the bluff of chalk, by the spring that never fails in even the driest of summers.

A pause here. The mist is lifting, the sun is a bright disk in the pearly grey, and it is going to be warm. The fitful infant breeze will grow up into a wind, I think. I love this spot. I have always instinctively understood why springs and wells have so often been seen as holy: St Winifred's Well, the Castalian Spring – so many others. They attract people to them. Without the gift of water we die. The spring is quiet today beneath the roots of its huge sheltering ash tree. Ever since I have known this village, there has been a rope hanging from a bough so children – and I might say not only children – can launch out from the steep scarp where the infant stream sees the light, its water as old as time, to land on the soft grass on the other side. At the foot of the scarp, held by the gnarled roots, there is now only a trickle out of the crannies of the chalk, at the end of this dry summer, but the water spreads into a quiet shallow pool with miniscule fish that dart from my shadow. Beer cans. A dustbin. Plastic bags of rubbish. A trainer. A broken chair, chucked down the scarp from the little road above. Hardly the votive offerings of the past. But a place where I can't help but find myself clumsily giving thanks, a sort of delight trickling through my rooted annoyance at the messiness people leave. (Console yourself: if people did not chuck rubbish away archaeologists would be out of a job.)

But press on, past the spectacular, fine Perpendicular church – but I am not church crawling today, and it is still too early for the service – along the old sunken lane called Mandeville. Was this where Geoffrey got the arrow wound that killed him? (He died excommunicate, and even the abbey he founded at Walden would not bury him. In the end the Templars did, at the Temple in London. Once, in that church my beloved and I stumbled upon his effigy: he once knew the land where we have made our home.) Past where the doctor, a fine naturalist, used to live, and then a chunk of moderately deplorable *urbs in rure,* (I remember all this as fields) and along the road over the bridge that spans where the railway used to be. I turn onto a long track between hedges rich in blackberries and sloes. It is a good blackberry year and an extraordinary sloe one. The day is getting warm, and the bi-colour green of the ivy tods, heavy and buxom like well-risen bread, gives off the sweetish, pungent, overwhelming, smell of the flowers. They are now at their zenith. Bumble bees and honeybees (too few) tumble and fumble them, each flower bending slightly under the little weight. Swallows are hawking for insects along the hedges. They will be off on their own journey soon.

This track I used to know well: it takes you in the end, if you can find the way, to a secret little place, once a village, where you drop down a chestnut-fringed meadow to a hodgepodge of a house, with bits of pre-Reformation ecclesiastical building melded to the memory of Georgian, and fishponds, now dry, where once carp would have come to the call. To the north, a little church, patched with Victorian brick. To its east, on a moated island near where the little river rises, stood the original manor house, once upon a time: now all that is left to mark that spot where generations lived, loved, died is a little, white, domed tholos, perfect in the sunlight. I cannot help thinking of T. H. White's *Mistress Masham's Repose* and the secret Lilliputians on their island in the lake. I read that book with Antonia, my daughter, a long, long time ago, when every day was summer. I have only ever been inside the little church once, when by chance I met someone cutting the grass nearby. We got talking, as one does. He, like me, had been a bus conductor on Ribble Buses in our native Lancashire in his youth. He paused in his sweet smelling task and greeted me as a long-lost brother Lancastrian in the benighted soft South. He loved the church and insisted on showing me the bells, and the memorials (Pevsner rates them highly) of the Cotton family and talked of the mediaeval landowners as if they were his relatives. The dignity of tombs and memorials overlays the indignity of death. Fragments of mediaeval glass in the windows turn the sunlight into splinters of stories. A grandiose black chair sits in the chancel. It came from India with one of the scions of the house, who worked for the East India Company. Little elephants with ivory tusks form its arms. The soft clunch of the porch walls is covered with more carved graffiti than I have ever seen in one place: names, initials, dates, some carved with a real feeling for proportion and letter forms. They range from the seventeenth to the twentieth centuries, when there was a wartime RAF station nearby, and I always muse about why they were carved, what stories they tell, and *how,* letter cutting being slow even in clunch, the people had time to do it. Was this some special place where you marked a rite of passage? Some initials seem to be paired: was this where young folk marked their marriage in the long years long ago when marriages were solemnised outside the church door? I don't know, and nobody has been able to tell me. In spring, snowdrops carpet the churchyard, piercing the leaf mould of other ancient springs. The place sleeps, still holy if empty to our sight. In a hole in the north wall a tawny owl nests. 'Wait for the early owl.' But Athene's bird of wisdom tends to fly only when things are getting so dark that people cannot see.

But I did not go to that place this time, except in memory. Perhaps I shall never go again. For where the paths crossed, my way was barred, by gates and notices that never used to be there. 'Keep out'; 'Private Road'; 'No Public Right of Way'. The thought occurred to me that we *are* barred from the old routes we have once trodden and loved, for that was then and then is not now: we have a new road beckoning ever before us. But I was grumpy as I had to retrace my steps – another lesson, for that is a good way of exercising patience, which is not my strong suit – and tramp along a dull road into the nearby village, where people washing their cars, their Sunday morning ritual, looked guardedly at the sight of a lone man walking along the road. Two men on horseback, their knees high up in the jockey position, stared at me coldly and silently as I walked past their stud, where burglar alarms were prominently displayed. Oh, the burden of money, of owning things! I joined the busy road, and you soon get to recognise as they come up behind you the noise of the different car tyres. There is one horrid sort that sounds like ripping Velcro, and the higher the speed the louder. Everybody is in such a hurry … Round a corner, a Land Rover with a horse box (with a horse in it) is stopped, alarm lights going. I suspect it has just come off the roaring Bedlam of the A14, for a tyre had gone on the trailer. A fat youth in camouflage trousers was looking ineffective at the side of the road. His mother is on her mobile, and as I go past I catch, 'That's all I needed! Call this service?', with an expression of utter fury on her face. I glimpse the hind quarters of the big bay in the box. I hope it was all right.

Thankfully, crossing the road, the next lane is quieter. But more manicured grass on the verges rightly predicts more studs. More notices about security. More CCTV cameras. More immaculate houses. The smell of money. Opulent cars. (But pitiably low wages for the stable hands.) A Lamborghini goes past. Elegant animals graze in the paddocks: pretty useless creatures except for racing. (It is not their fault.) It is a relief to see a little herd of Limousin bullocks in another field. One of them is on its own, some way away from the others: there is always one at the bottom of the heap in any herd, even human. They all stop grazing, and look fixedly at me, their big ears forward, their smooth pink noses scenting me as they thoughtfully (perhaps:

pardonable anthropomorphism) chew their cud. One, bolder than the rest, begins a slow walk, his brisket swaying, towards me to see what this strange creature might be. The others follow, and soon they are jostling at the gate, lifting their wet muzzles to sniff my outstretched hand, the whites of their eyes showing. But only one dares to let me stroke the short fur – the others back away. I like bullocks: and these are, literally, in clover.

With relief, I leave even this quieter road and branch off down a field path besides a long boundary wall, in kindly old red brick, with the black-green holm oaks hanging their dark furrowed boughs over it. A big notice on the wall says, 'Keep out. Guard Dogs Loose'. The path turns after a couple of hundred yards to run past the front of the house: utterly desirable, double fronted, big white sashes, in Suffolk ochre behind a carpet-like lawn without a weed daring to show its head. Urbanity, a dream of elegance and civility. This is the house that owns the guard dogs. Below me is the weedy pool where the little river rises. Another special place, a place that must have drawn early settlement when, where all these fields now net the landscape, was still the ancient wildwood. Humps in the ground show where stood, once, the humble dwellings of the poor. The church on its bluff by the water, with a round tower the Normans built, remembers them. It is welcomingly open: 'Not Locked: Please Push Hard.' Inside, all is welcoming quiet except for the creaks the old building makes with the pressure of the growing wind. I eat my sandwiches, and tomatoes, and an Egremont Russet apple fresh from the garden. I read the prayer Rosanna has written for me. This is where my friend Richard worshipped, taken from us so young, so suddenly, so recently. I say the Pater Noster, and pray for him. Perhaps some people are finished sooner than others. But the grief remains for those to suffer who are still on their journey.

A long straight path leads me across a field as big as a young prairie. It has been under barley, and in this golden autumn low weeds are greening over the soil ruled by the lines of greyed stubble. The wind is strong in this open, now, but fortunately it is at my back. Dimly carried on the wind I hear the church clock strike noon for the village I have left behind, and I pause to say the Angelus, the courteous habit of which I am trying to make as natural as breathing. (And keep getting sidetracked …) It is a curious layering of feeling: for I say the prayer sincerely, to be sure, but am obliquely conscious of the antiquity of this prayer which I am making my own, the multitude of lips that have spoken it. At the same time I see myself as if from far away, from outside: the setting, the colours in the fields and sky, my pause and stance – my mind flicks to the painting by J. F. Millet. Even the distant church tower over the bare field is there. The moment passes. My left heel is beginning to complain.

I pass quickly through the next village, resolutely resisting the attraction of a pub I know to serve good beer. If I were to sit there for too long I should not want to get up again, and I should get talking as I always do, and I am now seeking silence. So, telling my left heel it is very lucky to be in a nice boot – lots of heels are not – and to get along and not to be a pain, I strike out past the allotments – some models of tidiness, other a riot of bramble and nettle, as always – for the next little settlement: which was clearly once much bigger. I am now on an old road that hardly anybody uses, and I know that after a couple of miles the tarmac will run out, and the track will continue straight as a die between old hedges and old trees for more miles. I can feel the oldness of the way. It does not feel empty of passing feet though I think nobody has walked here for some days at least. Once, from here on was a lonely, desert place. Heathland anciently covered huge areas where the winds, blasting over the cold tundra left by the retreating glaciers, deposited sand, sand, sand. The axes of Neolithic farmers – to get the flint for their axes they dug down to the good black flint seams in the chalk at nearby Grime's Graves – cleared the old thin-rooted vegetation, and the nibbling teeth of sheep (and after the Normans, rabbits) made sure nothing eatable by sheep grew again. Men cultivated temporary fields, 'brecks', for a few years and then allowed them to revert to heath, once the thin – but easily worked – soil became exhausted. In a big gale the wind would pick up the sand, and the sandstorms could overwhelm houses, even, they say, villages: Santon Downham was almost swallowed between 1665 and 1670.

The going has changed too. It feels different under the feet: softer, drier, quieter … No longer is it the chalky clay on which I started. Where the busy moles have cast up their little spoil, and the rabbits have dug out their scrapes, you can see a dirty, limy, light sand. When you walk a lot you get to be very sensitive to what is underfoot: the clatter of a Borrowdale path of broken stone imposes a different, more circumspect, stride, where you often balance on the ball of your foot; the yielding shingle of Blakeney Point or Orford Ness makes each pace – you cannot stride – an act of will; the clinginess and slipperiness of wet clay tires before you have even started; the good quiet limestone turf of the Craven Limestone in season bathes you in scent and puts a Spring in your step. The bent Scots pines along this sandy track are only recent arrivals, planted since the eighteenth century to make windbreaks against the sandstorms. I like them, their scaly bark and their dark needles. They hiss in this wind, which is strengthening, and the sky now is looking threatening. I thought this morning, when the sun at last got through the mist, that the day was too bright to last. On each side of the path huge stubble fields undulate to the horizon. I pass into a green shade where big oaks lean across the path, and the underwood of bramble and hazel and ivy luxuriate. The wind is stilled here.

I sat down beneath an oak to eat my last sandwich, for soon I should be coming to a road, and then the village where the stage for this day stops. No harm in a brief break. But soon it is time to get going again, and the old path joins a tree-shaded road into the village. I walk past the pub, where people are having their Sunday Carvery: they serve till 4. A man is gently leading a very old lady (his mother?) with very small steps from his car to the door. There is a tenderness in his action, the way he bends his head to her, and holds her arm, which speaks of years of care, and the great mystery of love. He holds the door open for her with one arm, and guides her in with the other. I do hope they enjoy their meal. But then the door opens again, and another man comes out, obviously furious, mouthing something to himself, eyes fixed on the ground, his hands twitching angrily. He almost walks into me, and seems not even to notice. Poor man! Was it Richard Rolle who called anger 'a short madness'? Ah well. I am to meet Rosanna at the church, and must get on. Tarmac underfoot now: get it over with. A poster on a board by the Village Hall promises Messy Church – oh goody! – for next week: 'All Welcome: Children Must Be Accompanied By An Adult.' I pass a long, sheltered garden where some folk are sitting round a table, with glasses and the remains of lunch. As I pass across their field of vision one looks up, and cheerily raises his glass to me. I wave back. Goodwill, like sun coming from behind a cloud. Enjoy your fellowship: enjoy your walk.

The wind is getting strong now, and my feet are definitely protesting. It is only 17 miles, and they used to be up for more than that. It is with some gratitude I turn off the hard road up a grassy path to the back entrance to the churchyard. The church is set on a little hill. The automatic eye notices a bit of long and short work, the holes for the gnoma of dials on the quoin by the priest's door, the regrettable brick Victorian porch, the fine fourteenth-century west doorway. It is locked, firmly. It would be. You can't take chances nowadays, can you? Trust nothing: make sure you are insured. A couple come through the churchyard, with their dog, and are obviously suspicious about this shabby man loitering. They engage me in guarded conversation, of which the subtext is clearly, 'What are you doing and why are you looking in the windows?' I try to explain my interest in church architecture, and sound unconvincing even to myself. I seem to have run out of dog biscuits, which does not help. They clearly mean to stay here till I myself go. Finally, still slightly shy of saying it openly, I say, 'I am on a pilgrimage to Walsingham.' At that, they look embarrassed, make their excuses, and leave. As they go, I give the dog the last biscuit – there was after all one in another pocket, and the dog has been asking for one for ten minutes – and flop down on a bench by the memorial Sacred to the Memory of the Dearly Beloved and, as an afterthought at the bottom, to the Relict Of The Above, and wait in the wind for Rosanna and her car. What have I learned? Can I know yet?

And so the first day ended.

DURABLE FIRE

+ + +

It was difficult to get enthusiasm going this morning: Hector's usual couple of miles round the hill and down the Fen before breakfast felt a long way. The ground was wet, and sticky in bits. It is all right for him: not only has he four feet, but he can now settle down to a nice refreshing sleep before his meal and his next walk, and then another nice refreshing sleep ... and so on. It's a dog's life. But coffee did help a bit; and so, determined to do what I said I would do, and commending said Hector to Rosanna for the day, off I go, to pick up where I left off.

Not a great start. I felt dull, empty, as I drove to where I would leave the car, by the locked church where my first day had taken me. At least the weather looked as if it might stay decent. (It didn't.) I locked the car, went through the churchyard to the road, and set off. The first couple of miles were unavoidably along a busy road, and it is difficult to focus one's thoughts when constantly irritated by cars going by close and fast, and by the litter in the hedge, which was mainly Stella Artois and Red Bull cans thrown from passing vehicles. That was about all that road had of interest – but then, interest was not what I was supposed to be after: I was supposed to be pushing down below that clutter of the mind to something deeper, and it was not working. This could hardly count as pilgrimage, for I was getting cross, letting the surface noise be the only voice heard. It also annoyed me, while I am having a grumble, to see how developers have built – and they must have known what they were doing – a smart retirement estate on the flood plain of the river Lark. Take the money and run before it rains. Greed. And who gave permission? They can't have been ignorant of the habits of that river either.

83

But at Mildenhall's church, islanded from the noise in its green, I began the walk proper with a short, quiet, relief. In a couple of places the churchyard has been planted with 'bee-friendly' plants. Yes, the bees are few, and noticeably getting fewer: I kept bees for 25 years, and I loved my bees. It does not do to dwell, impotently, on what Big Pharma and Big Whatever are doing to our web of life, and so many in government and business knowingly collude – if they say they *don't* know they are either lying or stupid – in cutting off the branch on which we are all sitting. I went in at the north porch. There were no other humans in the church. After a spell of just being quiet under the spreading wings of the angels of that wonderful roof – 'Shelter me under thy wings …' – I pray for this wonderful world that we have soiled and spoiled, bad stewards of the Garden, and decided I would make that thought one of the foci of my prayers on this day's walk. It was not, surprisingly, difficult to resist the temptation to be antiquarian, to get out the field glasses and explore yet more of the carving in the spandrels. (To avoid that temptation, I resolved not to take field glasses with me on the next legs.) I love coming to this church. But being historical is not what I am here for now, though sometimes reading the building like a palimpsest can indeed put you in touch with ancient voices, loves and priorities. People have loved this place for centuries and you can feel it. Sometimes,

> what the dead had no speech for, when living,
> They can tell you, being dead: the communication
> Of the dead is tongued with fire beyond the language
> of the living.

DURABLE FIRE

A pretty town, and once, perhaps, prettier. Clearly it was once wealthy — most of these villages hereabouts were, on the fruits of fen and field. In the manor here Geoffrey de Mandeville was born, long centuries ago. There are ancient houses, but with unexpected shops: betting shops, a huge charity shop in a 1970s building which like a cuckoo nestling shoves aside the more gentle facades it dominates. There is a shop that specialises in car parts, there are lots of fast food shops, and many hairdressers and nail bars. (Are people exceptionally vain here?) There is a forward-looking barber's with a 'concept': a large chairless room, with plate glass windows to the street so you can see and be seen, and large bean bags to loll on while you wait for men in shorts with up-to-the-minute gelled haircuts to do yours.

More miles of pavement, through the housing estate, past the school, through the streets of sheltered accommodation, and at last into the woods with the sandy heathland soil and pine needles beneath my feet: and quietness. I came out of the first band of trees into a patch of open heath, and the first dog of the day bounded up, abandoning its attempt to excavate a rabbit: how do they all seem to *know* that I carry biscuits and will be *sympathique*? I nodded to the owner, apologised for feeding her dog without her permission, and passed on into the next stand, through the fringing thicket of thorn and bramble into the open glades beneath the canopy of the pines. Tall sheer trunks aspired to their dark cooperative canopy. There is often a strange silence in old pine woods, even when the wind is strumming in the tops, a silence that is just waiting for Wallace Stevens'

> Chieftain Iffucan of Azcan in caftan
> Of tan with henna hackles

to come by and Halt! at my feet. For the colours of the mosses, of the leaves on the brambles and wild roses, the bark of the trees, remind of the self-important bird, a bantam with ideas. (The trouble is that poems can so get beneath your skin that unless you are careful they see for you.) And here he is, damned universal cock! But no – though a cock pheasant does not make an un-colourful substitute. 'Kek! Kek!' he shouts as he rockets up for the patch of sky. He need not bother: I have no gun today.

These last weeks of torrential showers and warm sunshine have soaked even this thin soil, and there are mushrooms and fungi everywhere. You can smell them, sweetish, slightly musky. True to its name, there are flies settled on the sticky red caps of fly agaric. I wonder, can flies have a reaction to its psychoactive chemicals? I must ask Simon next week – he who told me that *Drosophila* flies exposed to alcohol behave exactly like humans at a cocktail party, with rapid, excited interaction, then a relaxation, and then more excitement as the second drink works its magic. The difference is that while we have hangovers, they simply fall over and die.

But you have to be careful of your way in woods, and be mindful of the lovely mazes you can weave yourself into if the way is not clear. Brocéliande, the magic forest where Arthur's knights wander into unexpected trials, is a real place: I have been there, and to the *fontaine* Barenton, where if you strike on the shield that may hang on the sheltering tree there, a knight will appear armed *cap à pied* to answer that challenge by the arbitrement of arms. All forests contain the unexpected – they are after all, etymologically, *foris*, outside law and custom. They don't behave, and that is quite good for us. So, indeed, I took the wrong path. It was a nice path, easy going, clear, parts open, parts in the dappled shade of birch, and parts again in the deeper masculine shade of oaks. But it was the wrong path. In the end it brought me abruptly to a steep, sandy bank by the Cutwater Channel that drains the winter water off the high land and channels it straight to Denver Sluice to stop it going into the Fens. It wasn't there when men first made paths in this land. There was no way to cross it. Why the path I had followed was there was clear from the little beach that had been formed beside the water: it was used by folk going to swim in these waters where 'Swimming Is Strictly Forbidden'. I thought I might be able to strike along the bank downstream to where the map said there was a bridge, and it seemed on the ground as if there was a path, if a bit overgrown. The first few hundred yards were passable but the nettles got higher and higher, and eventually I came to a huge, dense, bramble thicket completely blocking the way. And that is when it started raining ... It is no use cursing, you simply have to say, all right, I got that wrong, and turn round and retrace your steps to where you made the mistake. (Had I had my eye alert to the sun, I would not have taken that wrong turn.) You do not get on the right path by continuing on the wrong one: they go to different places. Nothing for it but to retrace, however annoying. Patience. Admit it. I lost a good two miles and an hour. And the overhanging grasses made my boots and legs thoroughly wet.

But that mistake gave me an unexpected joy, which without it I would never have had. I came out of the edge of the wood into a clearing and looked straight into the eyes of a roe deer who had not winded me. She stood there, stock still. 'What are you doing here?' 'I might ask *you* the same question, Madam.' Eyes met, while we briefly shared the same breeze. It was a glance into a different universe, almost intimacy across our two species, a glimpse perhaps of what might be, when the lion lies down with the lamb. But then she collected herself, and she bounded off, clearing the tussocks in high leaps. Envy … I had to trudge over those same tussocks. And then I came out from the next belt of trees into the area where the map told me once, millennia ago, there had been a settlement of men. In the open ground Highland cattle grazed. The men then would have had cattle not that different in looks, though probably smaller. The bright sun edged the wet grass blades with light. The cattle regarded me with some mild interest, chewing with that curious circular motion, as if ruminating really did mean thinking. Then, deciding I was of no concern, down went their heads again. I did feel they could have been more welcoming, and crowded to the fence like the Limousin bullocks of a few days ago. No manners.

At last, the bridge, and I picked up the droveway that would take me to Eriswell. I was getting hungry, and wanted a bit of a rest. It was good fast going, which was a nice change, and I began to work up a useful sweat – I was hurrying a bit as I could see an impressive cumulo-nimbus, hard edged against the sky, sailing towards me on the northerly wind, bellying with rain. Looking at its swelling bulk you could fancy that the Psalmist (ps.65) had one like that in mind when he said 'thy clouds drop fatness.' It would be wise to get under cover for that fatness.

I made it to the church: but it was locked, with no note of where to get a key. The north porch had a wire mesh door, which could be opened, with a notice that told you to shut it behind you to stop birds coming in. Fair enough, I suppose, but Psalm 84, one of my favourites, was here overly optimistic:

'Yea the sparrow hath found her a house, and the swallow a
nest where she may lay her young, even thine altars,
O Lord of Hosts.'

Not here, chum. Yet birds in church can be a real nuisance. One
of the annoying inaccuracies that one keeps encountering, most
commonly in churches with angel roofs, is that 'Cromwell's
Men' – it is always they who are blamed – tried to shoot down
the angels 'and when the roof was being restored we found the
grapeshot and look, here it is!' Nobody in their senses would try
to shoot down heavy blocks of wood with bird shot.

Birds in mediaeval churches were a problem, particularly
before many of the poorer ones could afford glass in the
windows. They remain a problem, and shooting them is one –
perhaps nowadays unpopular – solution. Their droppings got
everywhere, even into the Sacrament. And seeing two collared
doves cosying up to each other in their amorous foreplay while
sitting on the head of a saint, as I have seen, does have its comic
side in behaviour and context. So the old folk used hawks, and
then guns. The old list in the *Boke of St. Albans* (1486) runs:

An Eagle for an Emperor,
a Gyrfalcon for a King;
a Peregrine for a Prince,
a Saker for a Knight,
a Merlin for a Lady;
a Goshawk for a Yeoman,
a Sparrowhawk for a Priest,
a Musket [male sparrowhawk] for a Holy Water Clerk,
a Kestrel for a Knave.

The priest and his clerk would fly their birds in the church to clear it of the little pests: a poem of John Skelton's, 'Ware the Hawk!' (after 1503) complains about another priest flying his hawk in Skelton's own church in Diss. When Queen Victoria asked the very aged Duke of Wellington how one might get rid of the sparrows infesting the Crystal Palace, Prince Albert's pride, he replied, 'Sparrowhawks, Ma'am.' In that building, clearly, shotguns would certainly not have been the answer.

Oh golly, I am getting into 'mine of information' mode again. That is not what this is supposed to be about.

The cloud did indeed drop its fatness. Hard. The road was soon awash, and cars threw up great waves of spray. I sat quiet in the porch, ate my sandwiches – Rosanna had kept up her usual standard – while the rain poured outside, put a request for prayers for sick friends into the box so they could be prayed for at the next service, and mused. About the gift of mortality, among other things: what Tolkien made his early Men of Numenor call Iluvátar's Gift to Men. Bach's setting of 'Komm, süßer Tod, komm selge Ruh' (BWV 478) floated into my mind.

Time to go, for the rain had stopped and time was getting on. There was a path marked which would take me back to the Channel for a straight few miles, if I could find where it started. In the event, it was clear enough. It went into a Garden. (Like idyllic Ninfa[12] in Latium – going there seems so long ago! – it deserves the capital letter.) Nine bean rows – no, nine wigwams, for he grows them like I do, the canes in a circle and lashed together at the tops – luxuriated in long pods of runner beans. A file of courgette plants full of the fruit, and still with the blowsy golden flowers aplenty. A rank of parsnips waited for the first frost – they are much better after that.

[12] Which joy I have written about with gratitude in *Hungry Heart Roaming*.

Leeks stood to attention – they too need a frost. None looked too lofty in this commonwealth, all was even in his government. The owner was setting out a stall, for he sold his produce. 'Fair drop of rain, that,' I said. 'Yes, it wor,' he said, not looking up. 'More to come.' He clearly did not want to talk and neither did I. He had said all that was to be said in his garden.

The path led on past a huge pear tree that had seen many lives of men, and skirted his well-managed orchard. He had lined the wide path with young trees – had he only recently moved here? – that would bear fruit: hazel, walnut, plum, and at the end of his land, a young oak. I could not help a poem taking over my mind in this Marvellous garden:

> How vainly men themselves amaze
> To win the palm, the oak, or bays,
> And their uncessant labours see
> Crown'd from some single herb or tree,
> Whose short and narrow verged shade
> Does prudently their toils upbraid;
> While all flow'rs and all trees do close
> To weave the garlands of repose.
>
> Fair Quiet, have I found thee here,
> And Innocence, thy sister dear!
> Mistaken long, I sought you then
> In busy companies of men;
> Your sacred plants, if here below,
> Only among the plants will grow.
> Society is all but rude,
> To this delicious solitude …

CROSSROAD

What wond'rous life in this I lead!
Ripe apples drop about my head;
The luscious clusters of the vine
Upon my mouth do crush their wine;
The nectarine and curious peach
Into my hands themselves do reach;
Stumbling on melons as I pass,
Ensnar'd with flow'rs, I fall on grass.

Meanwhile the mind, from pleasure less,
Withdraws into its happiness ...

And I thought how right Marvell was: we look in all the wrong places for that which we really want, and it is right in front of us all the time. And I thought too how this is all men and women need to be content: food, beauty, unconditional love. How far away from what the world calls important and great is the work of this laconic husbandman, this steward of life and growth, of green and wholesome things!

Half-baked musings make hard reading. I kept on walking. I had lost my waterproof trousers, I discovered, when the next drenching threatened and I came to want to put them on. No matter: wet enough already, and it was not cold rain. After a mile or so I made a little detour to where the map said 'Church (remains of)' and found a pretty eighteenth-century dovecot in a field. But built into the wall was an unmistakable bit of fifteenth-century tracery: part of the church. When a village dies, as this hamlet had done, what do you do with the church? Earlier ages, unsentimentally, carted away the useful stone, turned them into cattlesheds, or just let them fall. The chapel of ease of St Richard in Reach suffered just that fate, and its gaunt, skeletal east window is the only witness to the small glory that may have been there. St Peter Eriswell's fate was kinder: to be a dovecot, even if manorial dovecots were loathed by the peasants for the damage the birds did to their crops, is not a bad end for a building that celebrates the descent of the Dove.

Rain is not too bad, I always feel, if it decides *what* it wants to do. Steady, and you know where you are. It's when it won't make up its mind and you keep having to put things on and take things off that it gets really annoying.

Plod, plod, plod along the river bank: some people do this path for fun. I did not actually see anybody, though.

+ + +

I left the river and turned into Lakenheath village. Boys on little scooters were elegantly flying along the pavement, making use of every little declivity. Envy: I wondered if Rosanna, and my children, would let me have one of those? They will not let me have roller blades, which I have always wanted and know I could manage – after all, once, when we had real frosts, I used to be a pretty decent skater, though far from the effortless elegance of my son and his Dutch wife who learned about ice when they lived in Holland. Keeping your wife and descendants from worrying is sometimes such a worry.

Once, footpaths crossed the runways where the vast RAF/ USAF base sits. I have heard that in the early days some people, determined to assert their rights and challenge the legality of footpath closure, regularly trespassed and gave officialdom a headache. Prosecutions followed: I know a man who once upon a time had been a lawyer for the defence. It was a long time ago, and the world got used to the threat, and the threatening, of annihilation. There was – is – a designated spot where you can go and watch the warplanes taking off and landing, emphasising the normality, of a sort, of potential war. A nice day out, and you see people with picnics and binoculars on a sunny day enjoying it. But could a war ever be a just war, if it utterly destroyed the enemy and all their innocent people? Was the bombing of Dresden 'just' – and that was not even nuclear? I have taught seminars in my time on the theory of the Just War, from St Augustine on, and St Thomas Aquinas, indeed, held that it is *never* justifiable to cause the death of innocents, intentionally or indirectly, if that result could be foreseen from the use of force. I can see no way in which nuclear bombing, even if a response, could ever be moral in ethics, equitable in law, or just in philosophy. These gloomy thoughts much preoccupied me – hard thoughts for a worsening day – and 'tis too hard a knot for me to untie. All we can do is ask for mercy, and not to be put to the trial, or tried as in a court. (Which is what 'lead us not into temptation' - *Et ne nos inducas in tentationem* - seems to mean: nothing to do with chocolate, wine or whisky, or other more intimate delights. It's much more, 'enter not into judgement with thy servant, O Lord, for in thy sight shall no man living be justified.')

Lakenheath village is full of paradox: the modern housing built outside the base perimeter is like modern housing anywhere. It is a sprawl of dull, repetitive houses on winding 'Drives' and 'Avenues' with little gardens which families have tried to make their individual own. Here is where the people live who service the bombers and fighters, and the bombs, and make war possible, credible, and they are nice people who worry about their pensions and the education of their children, and what they will do when they grow up, and have dogs, and get cross with their spouse and flounce out after a quarrel and come back and make it up. They have barbecues to which they invite their friends (perhaps relying too much on the English summer) and in the gardens in the rain the little domed barbecues stood forlornly as I passed. These people are simply doing a job, with little freedom of choice. Trapped, like Hitler's willing executioners ...

All morning, walking between two villages, the greater part of whose income now comes from the trade from the neighbouring airbases, I have been hearing gunshots. Now they are close. The base has a thriving shooting and fishing club, and just outside the perimeter fence and across the road they have a clay pigeon layout. My son, who is a very fine shot, has shot there. Where they shoot overlooks Lakenheath Warren, now a heathland with a number of rare plants on the poor soil, where I once spent a happy day gathering data for a friend by setting out metre-square quadrats and counting the species within them. (That was what I call a watershed day, when my mental world changed; that was the day when I first got interested in plant associations and the symbiotic relations between living things.) If you look alertly, you can see the recurving bank that enclosed the whole vast rabbit warren – including the airbase – in the middle ages. For this was one of the Bishop of Ely's most profitable holdings: as Mark Bailey showed years ago, fur from the rabbits was a proportionally huge item in his income. Thinking of those teeming rabbits sent my mind back to the pillow mounds in Smardale and my walk, another watershed, years ago across another England. When rabbits were first introduced, though, they were delicate creatures, who needed protection and cosseting. Then the rabbits found everything quite to their liking here, suddenly found they could cope very well indeed with the climate, and became a great nation, and bishops and others had to build fences not to keep them out, off the crops, but in, so that you could make your profit from them. The profession of warrener or warner was a responsible and important one.

This memory, and the memory of that happy summer day botanising while we heard the jet engines at our backs, seems to mean something. I am not sure what.

+ + +

By the road, by the church gate, was a big, clear sign: 'The Church is Open.' What a grand change from the normal! You feel welcomed, even if you do not go in. I did go in, shuffled out of my wet rucksack and coat, sat down, ate a Cox's Orange apple (carefully putting the core back in the front pocket of my pack to give to any horse I might meet), drank some water. I have always loved going into this fine church, and puzzling out its complexly superimposed wall paintings – fragments from at least five schemes have been identified. (The earliest, and most complete, dates from around 1220-30.) It's always got something to show me I had forgotten. I love its bench ends, polished by the calluses and grease of centuries of hard, working, hands. On one, a tigress stoops, beguiled by a mirror, for the mediaeval Bestiary said that the only way to steal her cubs is to put a mirror in the path of her pursuit. She then stops to admire her reflection, and the hunter makes off with her babies. The tigress, the Bestiary explains, is like humanity, the cubs are her soul, the hunter the Devil, the mirror worldly pleasure. But I forget myself …

DURABLE FIRE

You are not here to verify,
Instruct yourself, or inform curiosity
Or carry report. You are here to kneel
Where prayer has been valid.

I did, in the front pew. After a bit, I raised my eyes. Before me, on the south side of the Norman Chancel arch, looking straight out at me from the plaster, was a fine, near life size, fifteenth-century painting of the Risen Christ. Unaccountably, I had never noticed it before. Perhaps the time had not been ripe, perhaps I had not been ready for it. Its challenge was clear: 'Whom do men say that I am? Whom do *you* say that I am?' That to me is the most skewering remark in the Gospels. You have to answer. There is no ducking it. If you give Peter's answer ...

Which led me into another of those inconclusive reveries ... Do we make too much of creeds, dogma, observance, as if they were what the faith was all about? Of course they matter: but mere statements of belief or philosophical and theological definitions are not the heart of things. Nobody says the Creed with more agonised *knowledge* than the Devil and all his angels, after all. But the command 'Follow me' is absolute. No guarantees, and no idea where it will take you.

'Follow me' ... This church has a series of discreet Stations of the Cross, well modelled in bas relief. Before leaving I went round them, focussing in my mind the heart-breaking events of that terrible couple of days. Most awfully, in this tragedy, there are no villains, only decent men trying to do what they think to be right. The Jewish authorities were desperate for the people's sake to keep the lid on what they thought might lead to a dangerous revolt. Judas ... who knows what his motives were?

Certainly not just greed for money: perhaps to put pressure on Jesus, whose power he has seen, to take a course he just *knew* was the right one, by provoking a crisis? After all, if you look at the seating plan we can work out for that last dinner, Judas is in a most honourable position ... he was trusted: he was the Bursar! Herod was between a rock and a hard place: half Jewish, he had two fronts to cover, his relations with the Jewish establishment and with the Romans. Pilate, in one of the most awkward and strategic posts in the empire, is desperate not to provoke any more those pesky Jews with their inexplicable religion– he has already put his foot in it once – and to keep his nose clean with Rome. He has the unenviable choice between standing up for the law and justice his commission empowers him to administer – with incalculable consequences if he releases Jesus – and expediency. And at the heart of it all, the Sufferer, emptying Himself of all power and might, whose silence challenges, infuriates, overwhelms.

> Here, the intersection of the timeless moment
> Is England and nowhere. Never and always.

+ + +

The last few miles for today. I have not made good time. I made my way back to the Channel, crossed it, dropped down into the Fen, once marsh: the '-heath' in Lakenheath means 'hythe', the landing place. The path started well, but got harder and harder to follow. The rain was, well, less intermittent. You don't need padlocked gates you have to crawl under, squirming through wet nettles, at the end of a day. I found myself in a field with a horse:

the apple core would not be wasted. Or so I thought. I talked to it, as one does. I offered the apple core. It whinnied, but did not come out the shelter of the hawthorn under which it stood. Wise horse. By a lonely pig unit in among a clump of depressed looking trees, beside a field with 36 living and one dead sheep, I met a man checking his owl boxes. I told him about the dead sheep. He was not very concerned. He was talkative about how some boxes had had successful broods in them this year and how one had been taken over by kestrels. Several times he told me that, for it clearly rankled with him. It definitely lowered the tone of the neighbourhood ... Extricating myself in the end from this conversation, if that is what it was, which might have gone on for a long time, I joined the road for a dull trudge of a long mile or so. At the end of a day, when tired, singing can help, so, since nobody was there to hear, I sang. 'Tipperary' or 'Colonel Bogey', even 'The Road to the Isles', were hardly appropriate. So I sang the Walsingham hymn, praying for our loved England, Mary's Dower. It goes to an unexciting tune but has a good rhythm, and I could feel my stride lengthening after the long constraints of mud and tussocky, wet, long, grasses. In the tarmacked distance, along the causewayed road which is almost a lesson in vanishing point, I could see Lakenheath Station. Well, they did mean it, once. It is now 'request only'. (*Quaere:* how do you flag down a train?) Trains stop only on Saturday and Sunday, and then not many. The rain thickened, heavily, and was bouncing off the tarmac. A car stops, perhaps taking pity on this wet walker who is putting his best foot forward in the middle of nowhere. But no, it is Rosanna, meeting me, with apples to comfort me and flagons to stay me. And that was the end of the second day.

A day, alas, of inattention and grasshopper mind.

+ + +

The road past the station runs along a causeway: it has to, for the peaty soil has shrunk with years of drainage. There is little 'original', pristine, left in this weird Fen landscape, the most radically modified by man, perhaps, in the whole of England. In a field well below the level of the road, ranks of sunflowers stand to attention, all facing east. But they hang down their heads as if in shame. Their leaves are black, tattered, as our summer becomes memory. Their fringe of petals is all withered and dry, their gold all gone, quite, quite gone. Their ministry of heliotropic homage is done. It is the fall of the leaf, and it has come so quickly this year.

I walked into Hockwold – the name means 'the high land (well, it looks like that from the Fen) where the mallows grow' – and followed the long street to Wilton. The Church was closed: a helpful lady with an elderly Labrador called to me, 'the key is across at the bungalow.' But time pressed, and I am not on a church crawl. I'll come back one day, for it looks interesting, with (unusually for Norfolk) a spire with its base much smaller than the area of the top of the tower. And there seems to be a leper window on the south side of the chancel, through which the lepers, safely outside, could watch the Mass and be given the Host. That window made sense: for when this was the most densely populated part of England, there must have been a sizeable number of people with leprosy, and some sort of provision had to be made for these outcasts. 'Mesel', they called them (from Latin *misellus*, 'pitiable'), or 'lazars', after Lazarus, who, his sufferings on this earth over, was in Abraham's bosom while Dives was in the pains of Hell. Attitudes were complex: were lepers enduring their Purgatory on earth, and therefore somehow sacred? Christ healed lepers – but only one of the ten, and he one of the despised Samaritans, came back to give thanks. But they must be cast out – isolated – for fear of infection. Hospitals were endowed to look after them, often self-governing on the model of colleges. They were usually on the edge of towns – Cambridge probably had three, but only the Romanesque Chapel of the Hospital of St Mary Magdalene in Barnwell survives. Its size – it would hold about 40 people – gives some idea of how common was the affliction. (Cambridge had only about 3000 people in the mid-fourteenth century, at the top of the curve of population growth before the pandemic of the Black Death.) In the countryside they were often near crossroads or on the big highways, for lepers needed to be able to beg for alms, even trade in a small way, and in return would offer prayers for the souls of those who gave to them. The Barnwell hospital outside Cambridge was placed to take advantage of the crowds who came to Stourbridge Fair and of the regular traffic along the high road to Norwich and Bury. Getting a place in a leper hospital was coveted, and 'leprous brothers and sisters' were accepted fully into the religious order of the house.

That chance guess at a leper window (I'll have to check, one day), and the train of thought it provoked kept me going for a long time. I thought about how our quite recent ancestors dealt with a crippling disease, the pity of it, about their acts of charity and attitudes to lepers, about how they thought in a set of parameters which automatically included the moral, the devotional, and the anagogic. We understand disease far, far better than they did, and we have some pretty effective cures for what they had to endure with no hope of relief, but I am not sure whether there is not something missing in our default attitude: the efficient mechanism has not room for the holistic vision. Of course, my thought went round in circles and reached no conclusion, except compassion.

After half a mile or so, the route I had chosen had turned left, and had begun a long straight run north for nearly five miles where I could think without bothering about traffic or wayfinding. It was a good track, quiet, sound underfoot, sandy – this *is* 'the Brecks' – and it moved in and out of the shade of trees, occasionally opening up to a breeze from the east. That breeze was welcome, for the day was growing very warm and humid, and the sky had a dullness in the sunlight. Among the roots of the quiet trees puffballs were doing their slow eruption through the carpet of pine needles and leaves. They are still small in late September: I have seen them grow to well over a foot in diameter, and at that size they explode into a khaki mist of spores if touched. People say they are good eating when young. I try most things, but I have not yet tried these. I could imagine with butter and garlic and pepper they might be good – or at least the hot garlic and butter and pepper would be. Then I came into the deep shade of beech, and then young – but not so young, but they do live a long time – oak, and then a stand where Spanish chestnut were the main inhabitants, and the cases of their fruit littered the ground. They look almost exactly like green sea urchins. Few had the nut still inside: the squirrels and the deer had eaten them all.

I came to where the old road to Brandon stopped. I think the road was cut when they made an airfield here during WW2, and never restored the road after the war: you have to go to Brandon by some other route, and the old road from here on is only memory, and soon will not even be that. A car was parked in a sandy little bay, where the turning of cars had made and consolidated a declivity where rain could gather. A couple were lifting three very elderly and somewhat overweight Labs, in turn, out of the back. The care and gentle love between the species were palpable. The Labs – Labs seem to be everywhere, but then perhaps like other things you do not realise how common they are till you have them – waddled over to me, tails slowly going, and duly got their biscuits. (Not many left now for the next chance meeting: I did not expect three at once.)

At the edge of puddles, in patches of now drying mud, there was a lot of deer slot, mostly the little, delicate, sharp prints of muntjac, several only half an inch long – obviously their fawns. They must have come to drink in these puddles, here, in this thirsty country. I was suddenly overwhelmed by the beauty and intricacy of it all, and Hopkins' 'God's Grandeur' came unbidden. But he missed out praise be for puddles that capture the moments of the sky, for beechwoods, noblest of our native trees, for the scent of pinewoods. As I brushed past a thick hawthorn, a female sparrowhawk dashed away just at my elbow, in alarm. By some of the path, where there was light enough, broom grew. They love this light sandy soil. The pods are now black and twisted, having explosively shot their seeds. Those Plantagenets get everywhere, and the twigs are very tough, and do not break off the stem easily. When dry and used as bavins, as they used to be, for firing an oven, they flare up: the family temper …

Nobody was about, I thought, so I sang the Angelus, it being that time. But in the field to my right, just over the hedge, a Large White sow suddenly looked up from her wallow and galumphed off, snorting, to join her sisters, by the other hedge. They formed a squeal of indignant matrons, looking at me under their flop ears until they got bored, gave up and went back to their wallows. I felt a little chastened, for there are a number of studies (see the Web!) which strongly suggest that pigs like music. But apparently they like Mozart best, and put on weight best when they hear lots of him, and I cannot, I confess, compete with that.

I walked into Northwold: somewhere I had never been before, though the name had always drawn a sort of reverence, for this must have been where Hugh, bishop of Ely (1229-54), came from. He – and I am still grateful – extended the choir of the cathedral by six wonderful Early English bays, richly ornamented with much blue-green Purbeck marble for the pillars and foliage carvings, to house the shrine of St Etheldreda.

The church: Closed For Major Repairs. The noise of the builders' radio. I did once hear a builders' radio playing Radio 3, but that was a long time ago and it has never happened since. Two attack helicopters from the nearby base flew overhead, low, menacing, deafening, reminding of what Caesar calls imperatives. As I sat on a grave, as one might do, and ate the first batch of my sandwiches (which were BLT as only Rosanna knows how to make them) I remembered something I had not thought about for years, a 1960s piece by Nicholas Tomalin in *The Sunday Times* about Vietnam, 'The General Goes Zapping Charlie Cong'. And the horror I had felt was as sharp in memory as it had been when I first read the piece with shock. How do you tell a black clad peasant working in a field from a black clad Viet Cong? You can't. So you shoot them, personally, from the impersonal air. (But did Tomalin *actually* fly with General Hollingsworth? And if so, should he have protested? Or is the most effective protest to keep your powder dry and make things as public as possible? What would *I* have done?)

Russet apples followed, sweet and crisp.

And then I followed a delectable path down to the ford, and across the river to Northwold Common. Wet, lush, rich grass, swags of meadowsweet in the wetter patches, a sigh of rushes by the water. Then another river, the Wissey, and a bridge, and the long weeds in the water trailed out like green hair in the current, gently waving from side to side as the pressure of the water eased past them with small circling eddies. There was a late aftermath of hay in the field as I came up the gentle slope from the river. Rich land. Once, literally, to kill for.

I walked through Foulden village. 'A hill frequented by birds,' the Old English name means. But aren't they all? Why was this one special? A bungalow's elaborate and immaculate garden, with low box hedges meticulously trimmed in geometric patterns which spoke of hours of loving care, drew admiration if not delight. At the church all I could do was peer disappointedly in through windows, for it was locked. The north porch roof was collapsing, and was held up by a wooden prop. Indeed, collapsing seems to be what this pretty little building does well, for the tower fell down in the eighteenth century, and much of the rubble seems to be where it fell. The ghost of the spiral stair that led to the upper chambers half-projects from the wall by the west door – the door was once the tower arch. The odd broken windowpane suggests boys with air rifles. Standing on tiptoe so I could look over the window transoms, inside I could make out a few eighteenth-century box pews, some late mediaeval pews with damaged poppyheads, a sad, cut-down, painted rood screen. Grandiloquent, not to say pompous, seventeenth and eighteenth-century monuments, which would overwhelm a smaller church, sulked in empty silence on the chancel and nave walls, performing their proud display to nobody. Their worldliness seemed peculiarly out of step with the mystery of the screen and its painted-over saints: a symptom, if you like, of the change of emphasis after the Reformation from the authority of the priesthood to the pomp and power of the gentry, from the insistent reminder of the unseeable holy in image and paint to the matter of fact of worldly status and achievement. And now, emptiness and silence, and each week the clatter of the dutiful lawnmower keeping the churchyard more or less tidy outside. Sad.

And so to the last stage, for today. The day had got still warmer and still closer. I was sweating as I went into the bushy waste of Foulden Common. The air was still and oppressive, as if vaguely threatening rain. The Common is a SSSI of European importance, for its ponds are the relics of pingos, which still hold some sub-artic fauna and flora. On a day like this, it was difficult to think of sub-arctic plant associations here – just as it had been all those years ago botanising on Lakenheath Warren training for a spell of botanical research in Spitsbergen. (Sounds grand; in reality I was a gopher and dogsbody for the real botanists.) I plodded on, not enjoying myself very much and beginning to get a wee bit grumpy. I came out of the thickets and rejoined the road, which ran past a long line of grand old beeches, planted by a great estate centuries ago. (Who? Why? But thank you, thank you, for making the world more beautiful.) And so, on into Gooderstone, the *tun* of Gutthere, who is long forgotten except for the name he gave this place – like so many men, like Kraki, whose only memory now is also a placename. Whose was it before him?

'Open', said the church. But first, a walk round outside, duly noting – old habits die hard – the excellent scratch dial high up on the angle of the nave wall still complete with its iron gnomon. And then a rest in the porch, sitting on the stone bench along the wall. I took off my hot boots. My socks made damp sweaty marks on the cool stone. Another sandwich, a drink, and an apple ... cool down, quieten. After a few minutes of grateful reverie, I tried the old latch on the door. Open. Inside, wonderful, joyful, Perpendicular windows let in a sharp north light, and pews with intricate open carved backrests shone with the polish of centuries of bottoms and backs. (But alas, they had lost their bench ends, sawn off by some enthusiast at some point.) A good fifteenth-century screen had been more lucky. The painted saints were clearly visible, each Apostle holding a label with 'his' clause of the Creed on it in crabbed Latin. I said prayers for England, and for the rulers and mighty of the world, little men in giant's robes. Blessed Mary, intercede for us.

I came out much refreshed, in more calm of mind. A man in gumboots was going past with flowers for a grave. I guessed it was his wife's, for the flowers he replaced were fresh, and the date – I looked later – was recent. As he came back he asked me if I had come far. 'No,' I said, 'I am still at the beginning of the journey.' He looked at me a bit oddly, so to ease a moment when we were both meaning different things, I said, 'You have a lovely church here.' 'Never been in it,' he said. 'It's always the same isn't it? I've lived here for years, but you never look at what is on your doorstep, do you?'

Then the elderly churchwarden came with keys to close the day.

+ + +

A grey wind off the not so distant sea brought a cold, overcast sky that morning. I shivered a bit as I hoisted on my pack: that well remembered Norfolk chill. But to judge from the gravestones, here and elsewhere in north Norfolk, people do seem to thrive on it. They use the cold wind off the sea to preserve their lamb in Faeroe and Norway. It never goes off. There is a Norfolk saying, 'The prevailing wind in Norfolk is onshore; this explains why Norfolkmen invariably speak with their mouths closed.'

Gooderstone church was a good place, a palpably prayer-drenched place, to start this next walk. Once more I found it open, and I began the day with a prayer that I might not be too noisy-minded to learn something. But sitting on those wonderful pews sent my mind spinning back to the times when they were made, and all the sorrows and glories since, and to the unhappy state now of the country I love, where there seems no common mind or set of values except a mindless materialism and joyless hedonism. Grumpy old man: get on with your journey, stop bleating. There is work to do. And, as a wise priest once said to me in Iona, 'where there is no cure let there be healing.'

As I made my way down to the crossing of the little river – I wanted to call it a beck, for it ran over stones and made a noise like the becks of my own North country – a man working in his garden called out, 'Have a good day!' Thank you. In the wood by the water Himalayan balsam, pretty at first sight, but invasive and a nuisance, had colonised. I had not seen it in this part before. (It colours all the raised beaches on Arran, and swamps everything else. They tell me you can make a decent curry out of it. Is there some sort of symbol there?) Then, the last bit of road for many miles, for I soon struck out on the footpaths across the stubbles and plough to Shingham. At one point the path crossed where a farmer had planted potatoes and had not restored the path: an unfriendly act, but I suppose that walkers are so few on these paths that he did not think it would matter. Walking over potato ridges is not comfortable, fast or friendly, so I diverted round the edge.

I texted Rosanna, who had a copy of my expected route across this empty quarter, to tell her I had got to Shingham. She was mystified: the auto correct, which I did not check, said I was 'Aging Ham.' Well, then. Shingham's little towerless church, dedicated to St Botolph, stood all on its own in a huge churchyard: the village, the 'ham' of the folk of long-dead Scene, of which it was the centre, has died. Once, long after that Danish lord, there were people with the money to pay for lovely Decorated tracery in the east window. Now, a couple of prosperous farms, a very few rather *Homes and Gardens* restored cottages, an expensively converted barn. It has happened all over. Near Beechamwell, not far away, the ruins or, more extreme, 'Church, remains of', of five substantial parish churches stand within a one mile radius, and the busy villages for which they were the quietly beating heart have disappeared into the soil from which they grew.

Buzzards mewed their lonely cry, wheeling on the thermals – if they deserved that name in this wind. A jay clattered into a thicket, from the cover of which it chattered at me. A stand of wood had a girdling garnish of large spindle trees in their blowsy autumn finery. If anything, their colour choice now is even more vulgar than what they wear in spring. But vulgarity is pardonable when it provides refreshment for so many insects and their predators.

Over the road to the next path, and suddenly I am in the midst of activity. Pigs root and wallow by their shelters. Men on huge tractors are busy, moving pig shelters from one place to another across a vast field. Everything is big, sows, field, tractors, even the stand of maize through which the path takes me is over my head. It's game cover, and full of teenage pheasants. By contrast, a flutter of tiny goldfinches is feeding in the last of the rape crop at the edge of the field, and a few blue chicory flowers remind of the summer sky.

I lost my badly-marked path in among those pigs, and had to make a long diversion along the side of another patch of game cover to pick it up again. The gamekeeper was checking his feeders, and spreading corn for his birds. His job depends on how well he keeps his birds, how well and fast they fly, and how many he can put over the guns on shoot days through the season. (And an awful lot are missed.) We exchanged a few pleasantries, and I told him about the steep wooded cloughs on the side of Middleton Fell where I shoot, and how fast the birds go, and we agreed about the extreme skill needed for driven partridges in this open, more or less flat country. Then he asked, 'Where are you going? Don't see many walkers here.' 'Walsingham, a pilgrimage', I said. His face suddenly broke into a lovely smile. 'Well done. Enjoy it.' With that, almost a blessing, I was on my way.

They had been lifting carrots on the next field. Many were just strewn about, and would be wasted. They were all beautiful, perfect of shape and elegant of length – how I wish mine were! – which is why they grow them on this soft soil, even though they need expensive irrigation. And that water is often extracted from boreholes into a dropping water table, and the rivers in East Anglia are getting shorter. It seems daft, long term, to wreck a water balance and all that depends on it for the sake of regular shaped carrots. 'That's what people want ...' My envy of the beauty of these carrots is quietened by the thought that they will be full of the chemicals I refuse to use.

The miles went by. I sang the Angelus, at noon – I had remembered – as I tramped along. I came to a lonely farm at the edge of the forest. Depressed-looking piebald horses on a poor, nettle-patched, overgrazed pasture looked up as I came out of the trees, but made no move. In the field on the other side of the track, with docks and thistles overspread, by a hollow with a puddle, the white Emden geese were suddenly alert. I like geese, and I loved keeping them years ago. I love their intelligence, their cleverness, their occasional mischief, their lovely blue eyes, their dignity. They are social beings, and true to form, when I first spotted them, they were all heads down feeding except for one which was, as usual, head up, on guard. Immediately he alerted them and they all suspiciously watched me out of sight. Clever birds and great watchdogs. I suppose in this remote spot you might need watchers to alert you to strangers.

Yet, remote as it was for a habitation, it would have seen plenty of folk in the old days, the days when Norfolk was the richest and most densely populated area of England, the days when the Eastern counties and the Cotswolds grew the wealth of England on the backs of their sheep. That wealth shows in church and merchant house, in endowments and charities. The old tracks were highways between places now all quiet, places that hear no longer the calls of ewe to lamb, of gathering flocks at nightfall. Along them the slow flocks would be driven, grazing as they went, or strings of packhorses with woolsacks on their backs would score the paths into deep ruts. They were not quiet, mere footpaths for a pleasant amble, but the sinews of commerce, the arteries of news and new things, places where a walker on his own would be exceptional, even when there were villages roughly every two miles. You can sense the many who have passed this way. And now I, who have walked for the best part of a day on this old way, meet no other wayfarer, see no other boot marks in the wetter patches.

The ways I was following eventually brought me through the woods to where the west-bound modern road joins the line of the old Roman road that passes Castle Acre. I crossed the tarmac: it smelt. Until you have been away from the urban ubiquity of tarmac you don't realise how much it smells, how much traffic smells – as I recall my surprise at that downwind whiff of the M6 all those years ago when I walked to the Irish Sea. Across the road was a small plantation and in it, just before I came out of the trees and joined the green Roman road running east, I found the Cowell Stone. Is it 'Bronze Age' as the notice says? As a stone, an erratic dumped by the glacier, it is of course much older. But it does sit where three parishes – Beechamwell, Narborough and Swaffham – join, and those parish boundaries were set probably in the Saxon period. (And during the centuries of the annual Beating of the Bounds, I wonder how many small boys have been beaten beside it so that when they were old they would remember where the parish boundaries lay?) It is also near where the Roman road is crossed by the line of the Icknield Way, that broad meandering track that runs from Salisbury Plain to the North Sea (and once, I am sure, down into the rich valleys of Doggerland through those forests that now lie five fathom deep beneath the grey waves). I paid my respects. Some pretty lichen has colonised the crevices.

The Pagan Federation has claimed it, on its website, as a Place of Power. Who said, 'When men stop believing in God they don't believe in Nothing; they believe in Anything.'? (Sounds like G. K. Chesterton. If not, it is his style.)

And so along the Roman Road – I like Roman roads, even overgrown ones, and admire the surveying skills and, more importantly, planning skills of those old builders. Nobody has ever been able to explain them to me. They had, those Romans, no maps, no compass, no bird's eye view. How did they *know* how to plot the best and straightest route across varied, often wooded, non-intervisible country between two points strategically positioned to control a hinterland? When Chester does not exist, and there was only a crossing on the Dee, how do you *know* on what bearing (they did not have bearings) to set out your line for the Via Devana from Colchester? People look nervous when I say I still do not understand, and try to change the subject. I kept thinking as I walked along the road that I could just discern its *agger*. I passed by a field of raspberries, still heavy with much fruit. Remembering the young Augustine and the stolen apples, I ate a handful. They were no tastier than other raspberries. Perhaps the theft was too easy.

I stopped for lunch where the old railway line to Narborough crosses the track. Not a great spot. The view was good, the wind now not unpleasant, the bought sandwiches tolerable if not as good as those Rosanna usually makes. But today she is working away, and I had avoided the rather dull sandwiches I make. However, these did come with a free packet of crisps, which she can never manage. But I soon found I was right under the low flight paths of jets from RAF Marham practising circuits and landing, and the occasional deafening roar I had been hearing all morning now made sense. Something of the same feeling of disquiet, of being in two worlds at the same time, which I had felt at Lakenheath, came over me. The bountiful land, the enormous resilience of the web of life of which we are a part, the good people, my even-Christen to use the old term, of the past – and I feel them to be so close sometimes – all that picture shattered by the roar of a machine dedicated to defence by death and destruction. Both made sense, each contradicted the other. There comes a time for all of us, I think, when we simply have to look the folly and evil and suffering squarely in the face, know it for what it is, and say, 'I can only do what I can do. All shall be well, all manner of thing shall be well.' How, we cannot see.

But my thoughts are hardening: if there is a time to keep silence, it may be, as *Ecclesiastes* (3:7) suggests, it is so that when the time comes to speak out, you can speak with more authority: not to speak out against evil is to speak. It is hard, very hard. Let me bring it up close and personal: my beloved grandson, in whom I take great pride, is an officer in the Royal Navy, unquestionably an honourable profession in which he delights. But as a last resort, when the deterrent does not deter, it is explicitly dedicated to the annihilation of men, women and children, animals and birds, trees and grasses, with whom we can have no quarrel. It might one day be his professional duty to obey the Prime Minister's Letter of Last Resort. Do I speak? Not peace but a sword may be forced on us, and a man's foes shall be they of his own household.

Lots of time, on these quiet tracks, to muse, to let the mind idle, occasionally calling it to order to give thanks for some new-seen delight. Thoughts about oneself, brooding on one's guilts and failures, worry about this and that, about futures that might never happen, wanting, dare I say it, to control ... make it seen, or make it happen, *my* way – which is *so* sensible it is perverse (is it not?) to disagree. (First clause plausible, second patently not so.) Peace, prattler. Just be grateful.

In the wide fields on each side of the track there was round covert after round covert: islands of woodland like coral atolls in a sea as warm as that which laid down the chalk of this land. In the woodland and hedges and field borders pheasants were everywhere, practising their rocketing flight when they saw me. 'Very flat, Norfolk,' someone once said to me, quoting – and I did not spot it – one of Noel Coward's characters, who gets the reply, 'There's no need to be unpleasant.' Not flat at all as you get further north, where the debris of the jerkily retreating glacier gives a rhythm and a lilt to the land, and the landscape can become delectably varied in valley and down and wood and pasture. The land was now beginning that gentle metamorphosis from 'pleasant enough' to 'pretty'. One thing I did notice, and in it I rejoiced: the devastation of the woodland of the 1960s and 70s seems to be in reverse. Tree planting seems to be everywhere. There are very few really old trees, and most hardwoods – and there are a lot – seem under 30 years old. There are lots of young hardwood trees in the hedgerows – and lots of new hedgerows, too, flank the paths. We don't always realise – the yapping media never does – how much we owe to gamekeepers and the game industry. Without plantings of cover and coverts for game birds, it could not be economic to plant them or even preserve them from grubbing up and ploughing. But once there, they also hold havens for everything else, from beetles to buzzards to the omnivorous badger.

A shriek of gulls followed a seed drill's path as it sowed next year's barley – gosh, they do it so early nowadays! They were dabbling in the sandy soil for grubs. At the edge of a wood, on a hill, a line of beehives faced to where the midday sun would warm them.

And so to South Acre, pop. 25, little more than a church and a few eminently – voluptuously – covetable houses. The once prosperous village has died: there can be no congregation. Yet the church was quietly lovely, from its hammerbeam roof to its humbly beautiful flooring pamments, which had been paid for by a previous incumbent who was proud enough of his gift to have a tablet put up to make sure everyone knew. It was empty, yet felt full, and, had I had eyes to see, probably was. A fine, intricate, early sixteenth century – just before the storm – font cover, like a tall and rather vulgar wedding cake, sits on the solid no-nonsense Norman font. It was proudly given by one Geoffrey Baker, rector of this place. A very unusual mediaeval lectern, finely carved in wood, showed a pelican in its piety, a symbol of Christ feeding his flock with his lifeblood. (Only 20 mediaeval wooden lecterns are known for Britain.) In the north aisle, behind lovely seventeenth-century wrought iron gates – where once might have been a parclose screen – is the big surprise, even topping the lectern: the Barkham mausoleum. Sir Edward Barkham, once Lord Mayor of London, died in 1623, and the memorial to him and his wife Penelope is magnificent. Sir Edward and Lady Barkham lie together, dressed elegantly, and so far so normal, if unusually well done. Sir Edward's will (I looked it up) specifies that he be laid in the vault 'which I lately made for that purpose without any name pomp or great solemnitie onely with decency and upon buriall lying as shall seeme best to my Executors.' Clearly, when it came to it, the executors were not of his mind, for funerary monuments are wonderful opportunities for expressing claims to family status, reputation, even property. The details of the magnificent tomb delight: flanking the inscription, Life is sculpted as a maiden, and Death is a grinning, shrouded skeleton. Hourglasses on each side sprout gilt wings – how this takes me back to the time I first came across Francis Quarles' *Emblemes* (1635)! For time does fly. And below, two sons and three daughters kneel – and the carvings are so well done they look as if they might be portraits. They are supposedly in prayer, but they seem inattentive, distrait – as well they might be, for, between them, in high relief, you look through bars into a charnel filled with detailed carving of the bones and skulls of the family dead, which seem be looking out at the living invitingly. 'Come and join us.' Perhaps that is what grasps the young people's attention.

Two and a half centuries before the Barkhams became a power in the land, Sir John Harsick, once High Sheriff of Norfolk, and his wife, Dame Katherine, were buried nearby, in what was then the chapel of the Assumption in that same north aisle. (The Harsicks had held land here at least since the time of Henry I.) Their beautiful brass stops you in your tracks. One speculates: did they die together, in one of those regular recurrences of plague? Sir John died in 1384, and wears, like Sir Simon de Felbrigg at Felbrigg, the full fashion armour of Richard II's day, and Dame Katherine's hair is dressed in the Court style of Edward III. At her feet, but not downtrodden, a down-in-the-mouth flop-eared lapdog glares at a surprised and disgruntled-looking lion regarding us, couchant proper, from under Sir John's tapered sabatons. Sir John's surcoat bears his arms, and over the couple's heads his tilting helm with its 'plume of turky feathers' (granted to him in the thirtieth year of Edward III) is laid on its side and his shield is reversed and angled in the mourning position. All well done, but … these are clearly portraits. His moustaches flow over his mail gorget, his eyes gaze sternly at us, and she was beautiful. But what moved me most was that he has removed his right gauntlet, and takes her ungloved right hand in his, and her left hand is to her heart. What I saw staring out at me from the cold latten was love. All that survives of us, in fact. 'A durable fire' as the old Walsingham poem has it.[13]

On the south wall, a more modern monument. What was the story behind the young man who died in 1905 aged 35, having been churchwarden for 19 years? 16 was an exceptionally young age to have been given that office. And his wife took over the office – again unusual – for a few years. When she died in 1926 her children erected a monument of distinctly old fashioned taste, but named themselves in a familiarity only general in a much, much later age: Jack, Dodo (short for what? Dorothea, as in George Eliot's *Middlemarch*?) and Irene.

It is a lovely place, not grand – never was grand, for leave grandeur to the parish and priory across the water and up the hill – but, simply, a place my heart could delight in. It speaks of love, the slow rhythms of birth and family and death, the holiness

[13] But was I projecting on to this memorial from a different time and very different *mentalité* the assumptions of my modern sensibility? Ought I to have been more cautious, remembered Larkin's penultimate line in 'An Arundel Tomb'? ('.. our almost-instinct almost-true/ What will survive of us is love.') Jessica Barker's *Stone Fidelity* (2020) shows that couples clasping hands on monuments – a funerary fashion almost confined to England – is often connected with power, with claims to property. Dame Katherine, heiress of the tidy property of Sir Bartholomew Calthorpe, brought his lands to her husband. And they did not die together: he left her a legacy. Yet…

of being. In the churchyard I sat on a bench ('In memory of
....), overlooking the line of tombs of the Palmer family. Once
they too were powerful in this place, like the Barkhams in the
sixteenth century, or the Harsicks before them, with stories to
tell no one will now ever hear. Their name lives, just, in moss
covered stone.

And so, getting up somewhat stiffly after too long a rest
and consideration of mortality, on with the pack, and down the
hollow lane to the ford, where pilgrims and pedlars and peasants
and princes would have splashed through the water on the
Walsingham Way: for Castle Acre was the beginning of the last
stage of the pilgrimage, and many spent their penultimate night
here. The rich and powerful crossing this ford on their tired
horses would have stayed as guests of the Prior at the Priory,
once one of the richest Cluniac houses in England; the inns and
the pilgrim hospices would have taken in the footsore rest. Then
as now, behaviour and motives would have been mixed. William
Thorpe, priest, examined for heresy before Thomas Arundel,
Archbishop of Canterbury, in 1407, roundly condemned
pilgrimages, for many the mediaeval equivalent of the modern
package tour to Mallorca:

'Also, Sir, I know well, that when divers men and women
will go thus after their own wills, and finding out one
pilgrimage, they will ordain with them before[hand]
to have with them both men and women that can well
sing wanton songs; and some other pilgrims will have
with them bagpipes; so that every town that they come
through, what with the noise of their singing, and
with the sound of their piping, and with the jangling

of their Canterbury bells, and with the barking out of dogs after them, they make more noise than if the King came there away, with all his clarions and many other minstrels. And if these men and women be a month out in their pilgrimage, many of them shall be, a half year after, great janglers, tale-tellers, and liars ...'

And like Chaucer's Wife of Bath, many of the single women, widows with legal disposal of what they had inherited from their husbands, would, as that shrewd poet puts it, cross many a strange stream and know much of wandering by the way.

The ruins of the Priory stood against the western sky, mutely eloquent of ancient power and piety, prayer and pride. Once, as you came up this slope, with the wind in the west you would have smelt the tannery and the middens, seen the smoke from smithy and bakehouse and brewery, heard not the voice-over chanting of TV documentaries but all the noise of a busy farm. All the great religious houses were major economic powerhouses and big employers of lay labour. All gone, but they changed the world for us to inherit.

Once more on the old route, as I crossed the strange stream at the ford, I could not help thinking about the thousands of pilgrims who trod this path before me, and of Chaucer's fictitious pilgrims – after all, I have lived with them for a good part of my life. Chaucer knew that people are never simple. The rascals and those out for a good time (no questions asked when you got home) would make up part of any little group of travellers. But that did not mean that Alison of Bath, say, or Robin the Miller would be any the less devout when they got to the actual shrine, did not say the requisite number of Aves and Pater Nosters. Just so (in my measure) as I began the climb up the grassy field where once the buildings of the Priory stood, my mind was far less on kneeling before the Sacrament in the church than on having a long sit down and a pint in the Ostrich. But the two are not mutually exclusive.

Perhaps what we beat ourselves up about, things done and not done, and the things we grieve over, how inattentive and unpersevering we are, are not what really matters. They are forgiven anyway, by the very fact of our acknowledging them in sorrow before God. Perhaps there is something deeper in ourselves we cannot see, but Someone can. That rich young man whom Jesus loved: he was a good man, who had kept all the Commandments all his life, but knew there was something else to be sought. And Jesus asked of him what he could not do. Did he love what he was, himself? And is that what we have to give up in order to have it given back? Like in love? Easy to write about: damnably hard to do.

I got my pint as the long fourth day ended.

+ + +

The dark is drawing in now as we move towards the year's deep midnight. It's a daft time of year, come to think of it, to be doing a pilgrimage, for traditionally that is a springtime activity:

> Whan that Aprille with his shoures soote
> The droghte of Marche hath perced to the roote …
> Thanne longen folk to goon on pilgrimages,
> So Nature priketh hem in hir corages.

Anyway, up well before dawn so that I can finish today's walk in daylight. Hector, disgruntled, groans as I come downstairs and put the light on. Sigh: 'Can't you see it isn't morning yet?' And he stretches out for a few more minutes before I take him out. Once he would have bounded up and gone to the door and said, 'Where are we going? Isn't this fun!' and his tail would have been going nineteen to the dozen. But he is getting elderly now. I know how he feels.

It's an hour's drive from home to Castle Acre, the start of this day's silent walk, and the road is hellishly busy. I feel so sorry for people who have to do this every day – and I am going against the main flow of traffic! Yet the outskirts of Thetford Forest are magnificent: beech leaves carpet the ground in quiet red gold below the vault of those noble trees. To contemplate those arcades is some unexpected consolation when the traffic slows to a stop, a brief reminder of different imperatives. The grey morning has promise of brightness later – indeed, the weather forecast is one of the few things I more or less trust on the BBC – and the wind will be quiet, at my back. But I am glad of an extra layer.

I parked by St James' in Castle Acre – an appropriate patron to speed me on my way. I popped in to pay my respects, and for guidance – not for the physical way, for that is unmissable, but the other more testing way: 'May the Archangel Raphael go with us on our journey …' These November days (old Samhain, new All Saints' and All Souls, newer Remembrance), as we walk forward into the dark and you know there will not be that many more winters you will see, the dead seem very close. The fall of the leaf … but so far, not much this year. For many of the leaves are still a tired green, shading to sere and yellow, and they are waiting for the overmastering winds to blow them off and chivvy them into little piles that will make the leaf mould of new growing springs. Kneeling in the (visibly) empty church, the loss of three very dear people years ago was suddenly very fresh. Tears pricked. I pray for them, for their forgiveness, and for their intercession. (But, said Father Byrom more than once, 'the dead are very forgiving.') And just this week we have lost our friend Fred, and Tim, one of the bravest of my old pupils. Rosanna is mourning her beloved Irina and Peter, whose year's mind approaches.

The Chaplain's powerful sermon in Chapel in College the previous Sunday was still fresh in my mind, and its memory prompted many musings. (He is not to blame for this next bit, which you might skip ...) I remember the stoical wisdom and gloom that runs through so much of *Ecclesiastes* or the Norse *Hávamal*: 'Call no man happy till he is dead, praise no wife till she be burnt' – which says a lot about life expectancy in that earlier age. (Bunyan warns that there is a road to Hell straight from the gates of Heaven.) Yet it is indeed only when the last chapter is written, when the coda is complete, that you can see the shape of a book, of a piece of music, of a story, or of a life – see what it has all been about. And that is not instantaneous: that seeing also takes time, for you have to grow into enough understanding to read it, as you have to grow to be ready for some books, some music. I have been comforted, and have myself comforted others, with that thought, that only when the last act is done can we know those we loved whole, like wheat being winnowed from what the kernel no longer needs. Dag Hammarskjöld's advice seems apposite: embrace what is to come: 'For what has been, thanks. For what is to come, yes.' Even so, for the duty of life goes on – as Douglas Dunn puts it, ('The Clear Day') 'the truth that waits for me with its loud grief, sensible, commonplace, beyond understanding'

I set off at a good pace through the pretty part of the village, and took a narrow road north where the school bus, going dead slow, overtook me. Symbolism there? Out of the window a child waved at me, smiling. I smiled back, wishing a blessing on her. She knows not, yet, the rituals of death and mourning.

It was, to be frank, a long and a dull day, and it was difficult to focus my thoughts. I felt what I can only call by that old word, 'drouth', and you cannot – or I, at least, can't – whip up feelings of devotion, and if you could, I'd worry about how genuine they actually were. They are a given grace, like quiet of mind: and I suppose dogged perseverance, just one foot in front of another, plod plod plod, is what we are sometimes asked to do. It certainly seemed so. There is a lot of Norfolk, and some of it is up hill and down dale with not much of excitement except the light and the sky and a few magnificent roadside oaks which may have survived because they marked boundaries. One can pass the time of day with oaks. A quiet day. Bursts of partridges taking off surprise the silence. Now I know that their name, derived from Greek, means 'farter', I see the onomatopoeic exactness. The Greeks had a word for it, as they say.

Yet though almost deserted by the tread of men it is a busy countryside: the crops keep on busily growing, and in the distance over those vast fields you see one man busy with a huge machine harvesting them, and another man with a huge tractor and trailer busily carts them away at speed with a roaring engine and flying mud. Two men and two hundred acres … once the men who made those machines would have been in the fields.

Happier? I know not. In some fields the winter wheat has been set and is piercing the light with little bright lances of lime green – the weather these last weeks has been good to it. The farms are in the middle of lifting sugar beet now. It is an unlovely crop, and there is little justification for us growing it when there is a world glut of sugar, and people whose only product it is get starvation prices for their livelihood. But jobs would go at the sugar beet factories, and all that depends on those pay packets each week, if they were to stop, and the unjust trade for which nobody is guilty carries on, and mud spreads all over the road and sprays up from car wheels. Nothing wrong with mud, of course, though some sticks.

The problems of finding and following footpaths are not to be underestimated, as I well know, but the clarity even of quiet roads with little traffic has its own problems. 'Ammer 'ammer 'ammer on the 'ard 'igh road. For sixteen miles. I got the rhythm of that almost as an earworm within the first mile, and I had another fifteen to do.[14] In the end – it wasn't actually that long, but it felt it – I came to Rougham. A fine avenue of limes promised a large house and, as with many estate villages, evidence of bountiful benevolence in the past. Indeed so. A Primitive Methodist chapel was bought by the estate in 1997, after 110 years of service to a much, much larger community, and as a notice reminds, it is now an artists' studio. A beautifully painted red Giles Gilbert Scott phone box has a notice saying it

[14] But then I thought idly what good country this might be for someone on horseback, and remembered quoting to my hippolatrous granddaughter that cartoon by John Leech in *Punch,* (May 31, 1856): 'Vet. to Proprietor of Lame Hunter, "Ah, Sir, that's where it is. It ain't the 'unting as 'urts 'im, it's the 'ammer, 'ammer, 'ammer along the 'ard 'igh road."'

will be even better soon. I pass the School, given to the village by a benevolent gentry. A proud plaque over the door reminds that it was Built for the Dissemination of Sound Learning and Good Religion. Now it is a house, with only the plaque and the large Gothic window to let in the southern sky reminding of what it was. The window's high transom would stop the children looking out and being distracted by the beauty of the world. Outside, there is the once universal cast iron road sign for 'school': a red triangle over a white panel with a flaming torch of learning in black. It too was freshly painted.

A little further, and to my surprise in so small a place, the Village Shop – so it proclaimed itself. I went in. The bell, not electric, but on a spring coil, rang like the shopbells of my childhood. Tidy. Not large. They had no boiled sweets, which I like when walking, and which I had forgotten to bring. The large lady at the receipt of non-custom hardly looked up from her reading, and recommended chocolate.

The church looked interesting. Pevsner makes it sound perhaps better than it is. But it was locked, which I always find almost a personal rebuff. A Norman door, certainly, and Perp. and Dec., but peering through the windows I could see only what looked heavily and dully Victorianised. I might go back one day. Perhaps.

The road got a bit more attractive as I turned towards Weasenham. From some fine trees oak leaves desultorily fell around my head, as if the trees were not yet quite sure about autumn. The leaves rustled on the road. At corners they made little brown drifts in which the little wind dragged its feet. I used to love doing that, and I used to be told off for it. I could never see why, because I always cleaned my own shoes.

Weasenham: there is something not attractive about the name. (Ekwall's *Dictionary of Place Names* says the first element is 'obscure' in origin. 'Ham' is easy enough). I hurried through. Lots of Victorian high red brick walls, of some elegance, lined the road and behind them, red brick houses of great size, much opulence and little taste – even if one of them did look Jacobean. I was perhaps getting grumpy, and letting that get to the front of my mind. But that hard tarmac … and that tarmac led me on to the dreadful A1065 for an unavoidable mile and a bit. The noise, the buffeting by the wind of the passing lorries, their speed – it was unpleasantness shading into actual fear. And to think that six of us once – thirty years ago – cycled that road on our way to Walsingham to raise sponsorship money for the village church's restoration fund!

It was with relief I turned off for Helhoughton – 'Helgi's tun'. I wondered who he was, how he saw his quieter landscape, how few of the things I could see he would have seen when his world circled a different sun. I walked on, passing the deserted air base. Last time I was here, on that cycle ride, batteries of sharp-nosed anti-aircraft missiles, with that dangerous beauty possessed by so many weapons of death, pointed at the innocent sky. Now it is a silent place behind its wire and CCTV, sheep grazing its thin grass – it's dry land, this part – and it is much given over to long lines of solar panels, basking in the sunlight like deckchairs on the Blackpool beach of my youth. From inside the fence a man in a Land Rover, doing whatever you do to solar farms, waved. This is, I suppose, peace as the world knows peace. But then I had to step off the narrow road to let two gargantuan lorries pass. They did not fit onto the road, and both verges were squelched. I knew the man who chaired the committee that recommended we adopt Continental sizes for our lorries. I often think of him. There will be fewer on the road if they are bigger, they said. They gave him a knighthood.

Up hill and down dale … I am aware I *am* getting grumpy. Perhaps I need food. At noon, I sang the Angelus – to a mewing buzzard – on top of the hill where the Observation Post was. That little structure is now smothered in the disjoining embrace of ivy. More buzzards mewed, wheeling high, high up. There are so many of them now. Wonderful, for there were none when I first knew Norfolk. One took off from a high oak as I approached.

At Helhoughton you join the valley of the Wensum. That river rises over beyond Whissonsett, then runs west before making up its marshy mind to turn north, then it thinks about east, and finally decides to grow up and look after Norwich. I quite like that irresolution, thoughtfulness, in a river.

I went to the church, dourly expecting it to be locked, but no. The door latch was blacksmith work, old, so old that the thumb piece had worn away to a stub of its former self, and the black iron was bright with touch. The old door yielded. It let me in to a wonderful, simple, almost ugly church. The Welcoming. Suddenly the sun comes out. Come home: put your backpack down. Have rest. Sit and be still. Take your boots off. The Lord welcomes you. Incense lingers. *Regina coeli* and *Ave Maria* on laminated sheets by the door. A Victorian pump organ, like the one I used to pump when I was a lad of seven or so at my uncle's church at Crosscrake and there was no room for me in the choir. Prayerful – you could feel the centuries of prayer and praise this place has heard. The ledger stones on the floor were in slate, so beautifully cut, but letters so large and swashingly deep you could almost fall into 'Sacred to'. The antiquarian in me noted without noticing that the chancel floor is much higher than it would have been once, to judge by the C15 piscina. A panel with the arms of Queen Anne has a lion with a goofy expression, looking rather popeyed, like Edward VII. (But he did not stick his tongue out like this lion.) Underneath, an emphatic motto *Exsurgat deus et dissipentur inimicos*. (Ps. 68). It is dated the year of her accession. Poor Anne: remembered for a pleasing domestic architectural style – much of which does not fit into her reign anyway – and not much else, not her clever balancing act between Whig and Tory, her predicament between Masham and Churchill, her lack of friends she could trust, her many pregnancies and griefs with Prince George her husband, and all the time – surely? – that guilt about her father.

How do we learn to love more? I asked, kneeling before the Sacrament in the veil-covered pyx in its open aumbry, for sometimes, without warning, a wave of desolate realisation overwhelms me, a realisation with something like horror of how tainted what I have called love has been. By self. Is this what repentance really is, this devastating sorrow for what cannot now be changed, and which alters every future? You turn away from facing it head on, like having to drop your eyes when you can't endure the steady silent gaze of someone you respect or love, who literally sees through you, without anger or reproach, just with utter clarity. Just so the rich young ruler, a good man, who came to Jesus to ask what he must do to inherit eternal life, when the Lord calls him to sell all and follow him. Augustine remarks somewhere that Love is fierce, demanding of us not less than everything. 'Give me simplicity,' asks George Herbert in one of his most complicated poems, 'A Wreath'. But how do we escape the script that has brought us to that point of desolate understanding?

CROSSROAD

Where there can be no cure, let there be healing: a wise woman said that to me in the dark of a little church in Scotland as an Autumn storm beat at the door and bayed round the roof. We cannot undo what we have done. But again that thought comes: the dead are very forgiving. Be welcome.

> Love bade me welcome; yet my soul drew back,
>   Guilty of dust and sin.
> But quick-eyed Love, observing me grow slack
>   From my first entrance in,
> Drew nearer to me, sweetly questioning
>   If I lack'd anything.
> 'A guest,' I answer'd, 'worthy to be here:'
>   Love said, 'You shall be he.'
> 'I, the unkind, ungrateful? Ah, my dear,
>   I cannot look on Thee.'
> Love took my hand and smiling did reply,
>   'Who made the eyes but I?'
> 'Truth, Lord; but I have marr'd them: let my shame
>   Go where it doth deserve.'
> 'And know you not,' says Love, 'Who bore the blame?'
>   'My dear, then I will serve.'
> 'You must sit down,' says Love, 'and taste my meat.'
>   So I did sit and eat.

I said prayers for Fred and brave, stoical Tim, for whom I could have done so much more. And so too for that lengthening list of those I have known and loved. And was newly aware of, grateful for, small miracles, even that of walking, being *able* to walk.

A much better mood after that church, as if a switch had

been thrown. The hedges held a new delight, yet they were no different from those of the morning. The trees had a new glory, and the works of men's hands a new shine. The turned earth behind the shining ploughshare looked good enough to eat. The following gulls were miracles of gracefulness. The whiff of silage I got on the wind was – well, I know why cattle find it irresistible, and that is before you think of the alcohol content. I loved the delectable Queen Anne house by the bridge, with the river running through its garden, a weir, and a Chinese bridge, and a life size statue of Juno. (Thank Heaven, not yet another *Venus pudica*.) Somehow, she seemed a better goddess to face a Queen Anne façade. And a big fish turned in the water, a soundless whirl.

On to Shereford. The round tower has a rather daft-looking 1970s roof, a sort of outsize pan lid, on top. It keeps the rain off, though. I went in, carefully closing the bird screen as the notice asked. Where once the north aisle had been showed in the now blanked in arches of the arcade. Then, I heard a flutter, and to my sorrow there was a wren up by the altar, trapped. It had probably got in through a missing diamond pane in one of the clear windows. As I moved, it flew up to flutter desperately against the window. Nothing, alas, I could do. Sister Wren, I am so sorry. To avoid flustering it more, I left, and ate my sandwiches in the sun on a damp bench. I took my boots off: my feet were throbbing. Then a car drew up, its driver waving a friendly hand.

'I saw you looking at a map, and I thought, he can tell me where I am.'

He moved with difficulty, and he told me he had had a brain tumour. He was lost in the churches of Norfolk, in a project to photograph every church and put it on his website. He gave me a leaflet, which, as I write this, distracted me to that website (www.churchesofnorfolk.com). His words:

> 'Churches of Norfolk is not just another site showing Norfolk's Churches, for me it's an aide to my life, a site that helps me keep alive and pass the day, not only photographing, but meeting people too, some of these people most lovely and helpful, but some not always nice, there is the exercise and then there's the history and religious aspect too.
>
> Norfolk is the county I have been honoured to have been born in 60 years ago.
>
> After undergoing various operations for a fractured back, stroke and lastly a brain tumour, a physio suggested I take a little walk each day! He meant the equivalent of the 200 yards to a local store and back. Instead I now drive miles in a pursuit of Churches around the area, not only here, but other counties too, and take in a steady stroll when getting there also! ...'

Eyes met: understanding; liking. He too had seen the wonderful tracery of lonely Shingham and run his hand along the ancient shine of the pews at Gooderstone. He declined a fried tomato sandwich (my own tomatoes, Rosanna's bread, I assured him) and climbed awkwardly back into his car and was off with a wave. I shall never see him again.

I put my boots back on, and set off down to the clear ford that gives the village its name. I was resolved to wade it if the warning about there being no through road on the sign at the end of the lane proved true. After all, my predecessors would have done. If I took my socks off and kept them dry, and rolled up my trousers, wet boots might not be too bad for the last few miles. I have done worse. But, as I turned the sharp corner where the lane suddenly sloped down to the broad ford of the river, I looked over Wensum, and what did I see? Not a band of angels comin' after me, but nearly as good as: a pretty barmaid taking the air at the door of the mill that has been turned into a pub, and therefore there was promise of a pint. She seemed impressed when I told her I had walked from Castle Acre, and topped up my half-drunk pint without being asked. I flopped into a deep leather armchair, and took my boots off.

Outside, the Wensum chattered over its little weir – the mill was an undershot – and spread itself over the gravels. *Die Schöne Müllerin* – bits of – seemed apposite. As I came out for the last leg – so to speak – that red kite that had been following me down the lane, as it seemed, appeared again. I'm not dinner time yet, chum. Anyway, on the main road a menu of lots of dead pheasants to keep you happy. Pheasants never learn.

+ + +

And here I am, at the end of the last long stage, at Sculthorpe. The next six easy miles will take me to my goal. But questions are crowding in. What went ye out for to seek? What do I expect from arrival? That question offers itself now as it did not fully before. I know I have a curious feeling of regret at the approaching close of this exercise, for the doing is its own justification and fulfilment. The way is the meaning. And the return home: how did real pilgrims feel? (But am *I* not a real one?) *Fin de vacances?* 'Liars and taletellers all their lives after', as

William Thorpe complains? Writers of books? Are books 'true'? Or back to old clothes and porridge and taking the dog out and mowing the lawn and generally doing all the quiet good things: but with a different perspective on them? They must have been for ever after restless. I suspect I shall be. Here is no abiding city, here is no eternal stay. We would be at Jerusalem.

And so the fifth day ended.

+ + +

A day of (In)Conclusions.

Rosanna and I had not said much as we drove north, for there was no need. On an impulse I pulled off the road just after Castle Acre, at Newton, by the tiny Late Saxon/ Early Norman church. It has shrunk back to what it must have been – save for a dull Tudor window – before somebody built the chantry chapel of which you can just see a trace on the south wall. I have always loved its quietness and simplicity and I wanted her to share that. She was not disappointed. It felt alive.

This time, the last day, I did not walk on my own. Some friends joined me for the last six or so miles, agreeing to walk in companionable silence. I sometimes think one mark of friendship is to be able happily to be silent together with someone, even when not asleep. The walk's start was at Sculthorpe's huge church. It was firmly locked. The village has, in every sense it seemed, left. A vast churchyard with noble yews holds the many graves of the forefathers of the hamlet, yews which must remember the time before the church was remodelled in all that late Victorian confidence in the permanence of Church and State. We parked by the gate. The fairness of the day as we drove up had not prepared us for the bitterness of the wind when we got out of the car. Some dutiful soul working on the churchyard shrubs days before had dropped a pair of shears: the blades were beginning to go rusty, so I propped them up, to be visible, by the gate. The metal was icy. We stood around, waiting for the last friend to join us, stamping our feet, and pretending that we needed to look behind the church for architectural reasons, when really it was to get out of the wind and to have a suddenly urgent pee.

Gloved, hatted, scarved, we set off. Road at first, but there would be some crosscountry paths, and at least the roads I had planned to follow were the old quiet roads, deeply incised into the land by the passage of centuries of feet. Someone once said to me that all paths are a collective conspiracy. It is a nice phrase, and has a certain truth. We agree silently over time and generations to tame the distance and tie down the unruly land with the network our feet make. Sometimes those paths – as I have found out, indeed – may be forgotten by men, but find them and they do not forget the feet that made them. *Ambages pulcherrimae* ... you could lose yourself in these lovely wanderings of mind and body: indeed, both Dante and St Bernard warn us of the dangers in not keeping your mind strictly on your purpose, the hazard of being seduced into fictions or reverie. But it is itself reverie that took my wandering mind to their warning ...

We crossed off the road onto an old greenway that was once part of the pilgrims' route, and Rosanna and I sang the Angelus between the hedges at noon. Young trees – those good recent plantings, full of game birds and wildlife – listened. A buzzard mewed as we sang 'Amen', her alto and my bass resonating together.

I have had ample time to recognise that much of Norfolk is a place of ruined churches, for the most densely populated, rich, countryside in the Middle Ages is now one of the emptiest. The Great Barn at North Barsham, which is huge, has not seen a load of sheaves carried home in happy harvest in more than a lifetime: it is now a place for 'luxury winter breaks' and a smart place for wedding parties. In each hamlet, shrunk from its former amplitude, there are reminders of this impermanence of earthly things, even the best works of men's hands and minds. Just a week ago as I write this, I was looking in pain at Cimabue's great crucifix in Santa Croce, in Florence, horrified by the irrevocable damage done in 1966 by the raging Arno. But why should I be surprised? It is the way of things, which fall apart. At North Barsham, the west end of the church collapsed, and the Victorians built a new west end with the rubble. Just so: a king may go a progress through the guts of a beggar, one man's rubble is another's resource. Those Victorians built cleverly, I might say, for the stones have been laid in an interesting pattern and yet not pattern, if you see what I mean – just enough to tempt you into ordering and not enough to tell you you are right. But raise your eyes above the level at which you would normally look when approaching the west door, and two grotesques faces peer out of the surrounding rubble. Not gargoyles. They must be examples of those apotropaic figures of the uncanny, the wild, even the devilish, which you often find in the high places of old churches, defying the Prince of the Air. Someone had the wit to put them there, in this new old wall, a surprise. They look surprised too.

Mutability. It is so easy to say, 'Don't put your trust in material things' – if they are not ours. And the more subtle (and perhaps more dangerous) trap is to think that what you are doing (even writing this!) is *really* important – my perennial failing is to say, without realising I am doing so, 'Just give me time to get this done, Lord ...' Perhaps this is what 'Walk humbly' – a phrase I have always found very resonant – is really getting at. 'Thy will not mine.'

And walking humbly ... there is an enforced (courteous) slowness when you walk in silent company. Doing so has an odd effect on the mind, and your breathing changes, your body rhythms change, and the world seems bigger, time seems more plentiful. Perhaps this points to our human need, which we so often neglect, the need for time out, for leisure, perhaps in company. I felt we were bonding not only with each other, sharing this walk, this light, this point of reference by which however infinitesimally we are all from now on changed, but also with those who have walked this way before. The great pilgrimage metaphor of *Hebrews* XI does put us in the plural. It is hard to walk the whole way alone.

Perhaps we don't, ever.

+ + +

Passing between the brick abutments of the lost bridge where once the railway crossed the road, we came to the Slipper Chapel. It and the Roman Catholic shrine were full of lovely smiling people. An Indian family, mother, father, daughter, son in law were taking their young children round the Stations of the Cross in a progress that seemed as if to them it was as natural as breathing: the matter of factness of faith. But the surroundings, aesthetically ... the tackiness of the shrine culture and the devotion with which it is received challenges something unexpectedly unpleasant you find in yourself: the snobbery of taste. (So too with many shops in Walsingham.) It implies a scorn for others, a 'you and I, my dear, while They ... [complete as desired]' attitude which by any criterion is ungenerous, to say the least. The awful figurines and garish colours, the sentimental Madonnas (Madonne?) and soppy Babies meet a need, and nobody said good taste was a prerequisite of glory. (Or, for that matter, that heaven was a democracy.) The humbling devotion of everyday folk is everywhere apparent. And I was moved – challenged indeed – by the sudden shafts of Sunlight on the figures of the Madonna and her Son as I knelt in the chapel. Not a statue I would have at home, but bathed in accidental and unforgotten glory for the moment.

We had lunch: vegetable soup (cold, for our flasks were not really very much good), but welcome nonetheless. We sat in Eden: for the layout of the little box hedges and paths recalled exactly the layout of those hedged mediaeval gardens with an apple tree at the centre, and four paths leading north, south, east and west to signify the Four Rivers of Paradise. Benedictines – in habits remembered from my stay at Buckfast Abbey – moved about. In this wind their habits must be greatly comforting.

It was the ancient custom to remove one's shoes at the Slipper Chapel and walk the last mile to the Shrine barefoot. Some do so now. Henry III did that; so did Henry VIII on the two occasions he came to Walsingham before despoiling it. Henry III was unquestionably a devout man, so devout indeed that he neglected his kingly duties and for that reason Dante puts him in *Purgatorio* VII with the other neglectful rulers. Indeed, ruling is a rotten job, in which you simply cannot, with the best will in the world, keep your hands clean. Rulers, as I always tell my pupils when we are working on Shakespeare's History Plays and the discussion, as it will, widens out to broader matters, deserve our pity and our prayers, not our scorn. Shakespeare's great theme is just that, the cost of power, what it does to people. But Henry VIII: how did he think of what he came to be doing? For he was not an unintelligent man. Could he not have seen how subversive of his power – his job, indeed – was the claim of the Gospel? What indeed *were* the things that were Caesar's? Rulers generally get quite a bad press in the Bible: Psalm 119 says, *Principes persecuti sunt me gratis* – 'Princes persecuted me without a cause', and Psalm 146 warns 'Put not your trust in princes [or Presidents, or Prime Ministers] – nor in the son of man, in whom there is no help.'

We turned aside from the direct way to Walsingham, to cross the ford – I like fords – to Houghton St Giles. The little river Stiffkey is narrow here and in this dry autumn it was not very deep. Lads on trailbikes had been happily sploshing through it. I would have done the same, as the old folk might have done. But being accompanied as I was, we used the little footbridge and made our way up to the church. As we came into the main road, a monk drove past in a car with his warning lights flashing. A bad habit. The church – the reason for our delectable detour – has much surviving of a fine rood screen, but the bishops and popes and cardinals have been, literally, defaced: their faces have been scoured off the wood, even the gesso removed so the scratched wood shows. Real venom shows in those scratches. I have often seen St Thomas of Canterbury particularly viciously treated, his eyes gouged out. For he was the prime example, hated by the Reformers, of one who challenged the ultimate authority of the secular power. But scraping out those painted eyes does not mean that challenge has not gone away – rather, it shows fear of it.

Why are all secular powers so afraid of those challenges? Why do show trials try to get from dissidents a public 'confession' which nobody believes, least of all those who extract it? To try to stifle dissent is one thing, but to try to pretend that that punishment is *justly* deserved is to acknowledge the very values that question the authority of that punishment and those administering it. Even the villains, even the Caesars of our world, are caught in the web of the Good they cannot help but acknowledge. And their durability – the Thousand Year Reich, the American Dream, the lifespan of a tyrant – is as the dew of morning. Do they never learn?

> …within the hollow crown
> That rounds the mortal temples of a king
> Keeps Death his court and there the antic sits,
> Scoffing his state and grinning at his pomp,
> Allowing him a breath, a little scene,
> To monarchize, be fear'd and kill with looks,
> Infusing him with self and vain conceit,
> As if this flesh which walls about our life,
> Were brass impregnable, and humour'd thus
> Comes at the last and with a little pin
> Bores through his castle wall, and farewell king!

Back to the river: one more ford to cross, by the lush, wide, lazy meadows where the winter floods would spread their load of nutrients, but where now heavy, grey heads of autumn meadowsweet nod over the river, and sheep in sunlight graze. Appropriately enough: for the reading for next day, Advent Sunday, is about 'gather[ing] my flock.' We climbed up to the new path along the old railway line, a high and advantageous place with a wide view from the embankment over the sunlit fields. We could hear guns in the near distance – a shoot. There were pheasants everywhere, fat as butter, canny enough not to be near the shoot. But I have to admit that I think them generally rather silly birds, as birds go: they *will* get themselves up against a fence where they cannot take off, and a smart dog can fill your game bag for you, if you were to be so inclined, without you firing a shot. Our mediaeval forebears would have taken them with hawks, or with bird lime.

I watched Rosanna gathering the dried seed heads of umbelliferae: she loves their mathematical elegance. She stuck them in the top of her pack to take them home to decorate the dinner table for friends, and walked with them waving stiff above her head. A ladybird in scarlet coat sunned itself against the dry, shrunk, brown of the stem she had shaken. A barn owl prowled silently over the brown grasses and then the railway track began to rise quite sharply to the cutting through the ridge beyond which lay Walsingham. Walking along it, pace by pace, makes you realise that building this embankment, making that cutting with pick and shovel and horse and cart was a big job, however tiny compared with other railway works throughout the land. I could not help thinking of the dozens of lives claimed by the making of the Settle-Carlisle railway I know so well, and that memorial stone in Ely Cathedral to people who were killed in a railway accident in 1845:

CROSSROAD

The line to Heaven by Christ was made,
With heavenly truth the Rails are laid,
From Earth to Heaven the Line extends,
To Life Eternal where it ends.
Repentance is the Station then,
Where Passengers are taken in ;
No Fee for them is there to pay,
For Jesus is himself the way.
God's Word is the first Engineer,
It points the way to Heaven so clear,
Through tunnels dark and dreary here.
It does the way to Glory steer.
God's Love the fire, his Truth the Steam,
Which drives the Engine and the Train;
All you who would to Glory ride,
Must come to Christ, in him abide.
In First, and Second, and Third Class,
Repentance, Faith, and Holiness,
You must the way to Glory gain,
Or you with Christ will not remain.
Come then poor Sinners, now's the time,
At any Station on the Line,
If you'll repent, and turn from sin,
The Train will stop and take you in.

Where the trains had once stopped, we turned down the lane
into Walsingham. By the old station is the Orthodox Chapel
of St Seraphim, part of the same building being, somewhat
unexpectedly, a Museum of Railway Memorabilia. The chapel
offered an unanticipated iconostasis, and before it Rosanna lit

candles for her Russian mother, aunt and grandmother. We walked
on down into an almost deserted, quiet, Walsingham, quiet as I had
never seen it before. There was no sound of motors, only the steel
of my stick's end tapping on the paving slabs along the deserted
street. An ancient sound. At Common Place – how I would love
to have an address like that! How appropriate it would be! – I read
the notice on the Pump which told me it had lost its sixteenth-
century pinnacle on Mafeking Night in 1900. I did not know that,
and it is hardly important enough to remember, but I do.

And so to the Shrine, the end of all this my wandering. Was
it inevitable, this mild sense of anti-climax at the shrine? But
what *did* I expect? Glory and trumpets? Red carpet? Irrelevantly,
I remembered Julien Sorel's thought after his seduction of Mme
de Rênal, in Stendhal's *Le Rouge et le Noir:* 'n'est-ce que ça, aimer
et être aimé?' N'est-que ça, what this long walk adds up to, a cup
of tea and a piece of sticky cake, in a stuffy, dull, brick building?
Is the whole point of this journey that it does not have an end,
but the journey itself is the meaning? But that solemn moment
passed, as such moments do, and I enjoyed the cake, even thought
of another piece. Yet it *is* worth acknowledging – not being too
hard on oneself – that, like a long walk, prayer is hard work: it
runs counter to the noise of the mind, and you should expect
anticlimax. Be still. (If only …! The hardest thing of all for me.)
I can only say, 'What I make only so imperfectly make perfect
through Your grace.' That goes for people too.

+ + +

I have a lot of time for Father Alfred Hope Patten. He it was
who after centuries blew the small flame of devout pilgrimage

to Walsingham — it never quite stopped — into the blaze it is today. He had style. Some nicknamed him Pope Hatten, and from the pulpit of the parish church he would not infrequently announce that 'From tomorrow it will be our tradition that …', or 'As is our custom …' when it was not yet our custom at all. He won the support, and the money, to build the present Anglican shrine, to lay out its quiet and peaceful space as a new Jerusalem, with its Temple, its Calvary, its tomb, its *via dolorosa*, just as Iona and other early monasteries were laid out. In this space those wearied by the changes and chances of this fleeting world may connect, if they wish, with an eternal changelessness mediated through a long ago Event. It is a place sanctified by prayer indeed, even if it is actually some distance from the grounds of the private house where lie the ruins of the grand church built over the shrine which the Lady Richeldis built in answer to her vision. And odd things — coincidences, but what are coincidences? — happen. The last time I came into this garden, on a summer afternoon ten years back, there before me, wholly unexpectedly, was Father Timothy, Vicar of Preston, whom I had last seen at a dinner party a year earlier in Lytham and with whom I had begun, but not finished, what might have turned into an important conversation. (We were interrupted by circulation of the Calvados.) He looked at me with those strangely piercing eyes and said — no greeting, no preamble — 'I have long been expecting you to come and talk to me.' Then his parishioners, who were accompanying him on a retreat, claimed him. But I think that remark — challenge? — might be one of the things that fed into this slowly-formed, even vaguely reluctant, decision to make this journey.

Well, what does it add up to? I do not know. Mary of

Scotland embroidered 'En ma Fin gît mon Commencement' on her cloth of estate whilst in prison in England, knowing full well that there were those round her cousin determined to execute her. It is the theme running through her life. Her grandfather-in-law, François I of France, chose as his emblem the salamander, which she adopted. The salamander self-ignites at the end of its life, and then rises up like the Phoenix re-born from its own ashes. T. S. Eliot, who has been with me so much on this journey, begins 'East Coker' with 'In my beginning is my end', and closes it with Mary's 'In my end is my beginning.' The paradox is infinitely fruitful – like Herakleitos' 'The way upward and the way downward is one and the same.'[15]

On our paths, at each fork, our choice of way determines where the next fork shall be and where our journey will take us. But, as has been said by so many so often so wisely, we cannot cease our journey, and the end of all our exploration and our travel, will be to arrive where we started, and know the place for the first time.

And so I must start the next journey, knowing that it will be circular – no, not circular, spiral: I shall return to where I started, to the same problems, and joys, and fears and, yes, sins, but I shall see them differently, from another twist in the spiral. Wise Will Langland's Piers Plowman, perhaps the greatest poem of pilgrimage ever written, has grown inward and increasingly powerful since I first read and then taught it, a mere topic on a University course, decades ago, and it spirals round and round the same motifs and issues until at the very end the pilgrim has

---

[15]   Fr. 60 in H. A. Diels, *Die Fragmente der Vorsokratiker* (Berlin 1903), (trans. K. Freeman, *Ancilla to the Pre-Socratic Philosophers.*(Oxford, 1948; Harvard University Press, 1957)

once more to set out on the same urgent search with which he began: but he is not the same pilgrim.

Returning to this Homely House after the walk in each of these last weeks – yes, subtly I see what it is, and what it stands for, differently. Not everything matters. But some things matter immeasurably. Like that next journey, for which this and all the others have been prelude.

+ + +

We had a noisy taxi back to where we had left the cars to follow the ancient footsteps. The driver was a large, jolly, jokey girl from Essex who told us, 'I am just learning the ways round here. So tell me if I go wrong.' (I could say the same …) She kept up a flood of cheery conversation all the way, to which it was only courteous to respond. But the last of the light in the western sky is what held my eyes.

> For I have learned
> To look on nature, not as in the hour
> Of thoughtless youth; but hearing oftentimes
> The still, sad music of humanity,
> Nor harsh nor grating, though of ample power
> To chasten and subdue. And I have felt
> A presence that disturbs me with the joy
> Of elevated thoughts; a sense sublime
> Of something far more deeply interfused,
> Whose dwelling is the light of setting suns,
> And the round ocean, and the living air,
> And the blue sky, and in the mind of man:

DURABLE FIRE

A motion and a spirit, that impels
All thinking things, all objects of all thought,
And rolls through all things.

And so home, to Hector's glad welcome.

5

One More River

*'God made one of you, and it's up to you
to find out what that creation is.'*
Marilynne Robinson, in conversation with
Bishop Rowan Williams, Lady Day 2019

Holy Week. The yearly challenge, if you will stop to listen to the whisper: it is never shouted at you. 'Whom do you say that I am?' Almost at a whim – which is how big decisions in my life seem to happen – I decided to mark it by setting one day aside as silent, solitary, and involving a significant walk and contemplation, and culminating, when I arrived at the beloved church which would be my destination, in the Stations of the Cross. Once more that challenge: 'Do what you have told your pupils about … do it for real. See what happens. Don't expect too much. Or, indeed, don't expect anything.'

There wasn't time, in that busy year after my friend Hector the Labrador died, to walk again those old paths to Walsingham, to go to that place of memory and, perhaps, find it a place in whose novelty you are humbled. Work, teaching, writing, one thing after another – the Martha things without which the Mary ones simply cannot be done. (Or so one thinks.) Yet the call of a lone walk, a lone stepping outside the normal, was once more insistent, growing the stronger as the possibility seemed more remote as we moved further into a late Lent, the lengthening season, when sunset gets later by the day and the winter really does seem past and over. I do not know why I felt this call: except that the Walsingham walk, the first explicit pilgrimage I had ever done (though there were others that were I now see to have been implicit ones, perhaps preparing for it) had – has – in memory grown rather than lessened in vividness and significance. That memory of an old and the idea of a new walk kept nudging at me. Joseph Conrad says of the stories told by one of his characters, Marlow in *Heart of Darkness,* '... to him the meaning of an episode was not inside like a kernel but outside, enveloping the tale which brought it out only as a glow brings out a haze, in the likeness of one of these misty halos that sometimes are made visible by the spectral illumination of moonshine.' That puts my experience and memory (of many things) better than I ever could.

So I decided that, come what may, I would shelve everything and take Tuesday in Holy Week off and walk along the Cam between the Cathedral at Ely and St Mary the Less in Cambridge, the church that stood just outside the lost Trumpington Gate of the little city, *civitatula*, on a river (as Bede calls it). That is the wrong way about, of course, for most people who walk that route end up in the City built on a hill that cannot be hid and pass through the Galilee to enter the Cathedral with its welcoming, challenging labyrinth. Centuries ago, before the cataclysm of the Reformation, the rich shrine of Aeþelþryð (thankfully Latinised as Etheldreda), would have been their goal. I had my reasons, which seemed good at the time: the chief was to arrive at Little St Mary's to conclude this Holy Week walk and its opportunity for quietness, and even meditation outside the daily background noise of busy-ness, with the Stations of the Cross. Once more, as so often in my life, hindsight is a wonderful teacher: to write about something, to try to catch the polyphony of multi-sensual experience in the plainsong of words, is sometimes to see what you did not then see.

Don't expect anything … The 20 or so mile traipse by byway, field path and mostly tow path – the flattest longish walk I have ever done – from Ely to Cambridge is not a very interesting walk to one brought up in sight of the high hills of the west: a penance, almost, if you wanted to take it so. (Hills are more, well, punctuated.) It was Lent, after all. But people who had heard what I planned had asked if I was doing it for charity, which was *not* the original idea, and in the end I said I was. The sponsorship money so raised would go to charities supporting the growing numbers of the homeless with whom our self-indulgent affluence does not know what to do, or how to engage. So whatever the result might be for me, anything or nothing, I found myself with a responsibility to those who had offered support. And Left Hip – my inseparable companion, almost a character in the story, and grumpy quite recently – had recently been blessedly quiescent. But old feet hobbled me somewhat.

+ + +

Across the quiet Fen to early Mass with Rosanna in the Cathedral. A dense mist. The single track road ('with passing places'), dead straight but twisted and heaved and cracked by the shrinking of the peat on which it was laid, threw the car about a lot. You have to go slowly, take the journey (as too rarely I do) gently. The light is luminous, but thick. But this really quite dense early morning mist will burn off soon. It is not very deep – in fact, from the top of the little hill in the village you could that morning stand in early sunlight and look out over a white blanket of mist through which the taller trees and electricity pylons stuck out. But down here, the sun is a pallid, shy extra brightness in the whiteness. A cock pheasant in proud plumage whirs up exultant on triumphant wings almost from under our wheels, indignant. We rise above the mist as the road climbs up to the bank of the Cam wash at Upware, and there is blue sky, and the sun lighting up the far trees. A clatter of jackdaws – they never stop talking – flies over. This higher spit of land – the soil colour has changed – was a coral reef in the Jurassic. Here, where the lodes come from Burwell and Wicken and Reach to join their waters to the Cam on its journey to the sea, the Romans had what the archaeologists digging it told me they thought was a warehouse, stone built, substantial, probably to marshal the produce of the imperial villa estates round this part of the Fen basin. But that was a long time ago.

I shall be walking this way in a few hours.

Ely is quiet. The Green in front of the west door is deserted. We push open the wicket gate in the great west door inside the Galilee porch, where pilgrims would once have washed their travel-stained feet before entering. There is the familiar rush of air through it as we step into the vast nave. It is empty, and our footsteps and the tap of my sticks echo round the arcades.

A dozen or so of us gather in silence in Bishop West's chapel, lovely, though now only a shade of the subtle glory the Reformers wrecked. Behind me a canopied tomb records the remains of Saxon bishops and of Ealdorman Byrtnoth, killed on the causeway at Maldon by the Danes long years ago. Everywhere I look, as we wait for the Eucharist to begin, I see Nicholas West's motto, which he chose from St Paul (I *Cor.* xv.10): *Dei gratia sum id quod sum*. I wonder why he chose this. 'Hasn't God been good to me in giving me this plum bishopric!'? 'Haven't I done well, when once I was merely a little boy on the Foundation at Eton!'? And he has built himself a most magnificent and unignorable chantry in a soufflé of late Gothic structure and up to the minute Italian Renaissance detail. 'By the Grace of God I am what I am.' But I like to think he was deliberately ambiguous: perhaps it was real humility, just as the monks say Thomas Becket, proud prelate, was wearing a hair shirt under the magnificence of archiepiscopal majesty. Perhaps he is implying, 'I accept my faults, for even they can work to the glory of God. Even in my brokenness, God has a use for me, even that brokenness may be part of the purpose; yes, his mercy is over all.' Yes, but the mercy of God is no excuse for us not trying. We are his hands in the world, as Fr David used to say, and even dirty, clumsy hands can be useful and do good work. But then comes another thought: why do I always think that I have to be proactive? Why am I so busy, and uneasy if I am not making things happen? Do I not trust that sometimes it is as important to stop, listen, shut up, do *nothing*? 'Be still, and know.' All my life has been spent doing the opposite. Is it pride? Like the character in Steinbeck's *Sweet Thursday* who can't let himself off watching the sun go down into the sea each day because he thinks it cannot do it without him. But it most certainly can.

The Bishop's Chaplain gives me that gracious Irish blessing after the Eucharist:

'May the road rise up to meet you.

May the wind be always at your back.

May the sun shine warm upon your face;

the rains fall soft upon your fields

and until we meet again, may God hold you in the palm

of His hand.'

We are both moved. Rosanna sets off for her work in Cambridge, and I set off on my walk to get myself a coffee on the Railway Station. I give my cantankerous left hip, who has been troublesome lately, a strong talking to before I set off. (It did in fact grumble all the way: 'Not a nice thing to do to an elderly hip … No consideration … what do you expect of young folk nowadays? Mutter mutter …')

I sit on a bench, amid the busy people catching trains to work, with a curious sense of holiday. It is nice to watch the world go by … a colleague dashing along with his briefcase open to catch the Cambridge train, then another (one of the most learned men I know) clearly deep in thought, almost missing it even though he has been standing by it for a good two minutes. I don't have to do that today. I can sit and watch the brains go by. So I get another coffee and watch another train full of busy people leave in another direction …

Leisure matters – though I do it very badly. It is the basis of any culture – you can't have art and thought and poetry if your nose is always to the grindstone, or when you cannot straighten up from lathe or furrow – or, (to make the shoe pinch) from writing learned articles for peer review, which then nobody will read. Leisure is an attitude of mind and a condition of the soul that makes possible a capacity to see what the nature of the world really is – which we express so much through myth and fiction, not least the myths and fictions of science. The Greeks and our mediaeval forebears understood this, and built time for leisure into the yearly, daily, cycle. For leisure has been, and always will be, the first foundation of any culture. The (I think) appallingly neglected philosopher Josef Pieper maintained in his *Leisure, the Basis of Culture* (1948) that the bourgeois, commercial world of total labour had abolished real leisure, and warned that unless we recovered a recognition of the value, and regain the art, of silence and insight, the ability for non-activity, unless we substitute true leisure for mere hectic amusement, we would destroy our culture – and ourselves. Pieper also points out that religion can be born only in leisure – allowing time for the contemplation of nature, and of the nature of God. But of course such thoughts would never be welcomed by those who are committed to, or trapped in, the economic and political models that are criticised. It is so hard to admit you are wrong, that you – we – have taken a wrong turning.

In the end, fuelled with my double caffeine fix and almost wondering about a bun, I set off: under the railway through the extremely low underpass where almost every week some van would take its roof off, then a right turn onto a long, not unpleasant, trudge along the high flood bank. It is still quite early. The noise from hurrying commuting traffic on the new bypass can be heard for a mile or so – another reminder that this is a day when I deliberately stand aside from all I have to do. Here the path runs high above the black fields over towards the bluff of Stuntney, for the peat of the fen has shrunk to far below the level of the lazy river. Swans dot both. Some fields shine in the light where sheets of plastic cover them, and the wind occasionally gets under the sheets so that you seem to have the waves of small lakes scudding to the horizon. Once you would have had real lakes, of course, for Ely ('Eel Island') was indeed an island before the fen was drained, and the slow river then meandered very close to the abrupt little hill on which the cathedral stands. This explains the story in the twelfth-century *Liber Eliensis* of how Canute and his queen, Emma of Normandy,[16] travelling in their boat to Ely for Candlemas, were able to hear the monks singing in the church – it wasn't a cathedral till 1083. The chronicler then says 'to express his joy, he composed this song in English:

> Merie sungen þe muneches binnen Ely
> þa Cnut cyng reu þer by.
> Roweð cnites noer the lant
> and here we þes muneches sæng.

> (Merrily sang the monks in Ely,
> When Cnut the king rowed by.
> 'Row, men, nearer the land,
> And let us hear these monks sing.')

He then translates the lines into Latin and says 'this and the rest [which we do not have] are to this day sung publicly by choirs and remembered in proverbs.' It's good to know that the choir

---

[16] At the age of 12 she was married to Aeþelraed Unraede, Ethelred the Ill-Counselled, by whom she had Edward, later King and Confessor, who is claimed as founder by the King's School at Ely. Later, she married Canute, by whom she had Harthacanute, whom Sellars and Yeatman in *1066 and All That* call 'Halfacanute.'

of Ely was as worth hearing then as the cathedral choir is now.

They must have had an open February. On another February, again going to Ely for the Candlemas feast, the fens were frozen hard, but the king was able to get there with the help of a 'large and rugged man from the Isle, Brihtmær surnamed Budde on account of his bulk.' Brihtmær (who won his freedom by this act) led the way across the ice from Soham to Ely with the king following in a wagon, and 'everybody marvelled that he should have attempted such a great act of daring.' Along the route of the old timber causeway across the marsh, the shortest crossing from the high bluff of Stuntney, Stunta's Island, to Ely, the traffic from Soham thunders, the note changing as it drops from the high land to cross the peat.

Once again, as always, place names intrigue. I wonder who Stunta was, and why he was called by a name that means 'foolish.' Idle thoughts of an idle fellow … but the real people behind the placenames do matter, even if their stories are now unknowable to us.

My phone is on silent, but Rosanna put an alert on it for regular intervals so that I did not forget to let her know where I am, as I did too frequently when I walked to Walsingham. She thought it would only vibrate, but it in fact quacks like a duck. That is appropriate, I suppose, in this country, and a good reminder to stop, and think, and remind myself of the Passion, and say a Pater Noster and the Jesus Prayer. For I so easily get distracted by the wonder along the way.

For example, on the path are bits of a dead blackheaded gull. Fresh. It has conspicuously been someone's lunch, and they were messy feeders. So off I go into inconclusive, useless, speculation about which predator might have enjoyed it. And that leads me into thinking about Tennyson's vision of 'Nature red in tooth and claw', and Psalm 145's 'The eyes of all wait upon thee, O Lord, and thou givest them their meat in due season', and I get in a terrible muddle and nearly fall into a bog of theodicy. Fools rush in … Dinner is a blessing to the diner, but not to the dinner. Unless our model is woefully skewed. It may be. There is that old Classical idea, echoed by Ben Jonson and Andrew Marvell in two of my most loved poems, of *sponte sua*, self-giving,

> 'The painted partridge lies in every field,
> And for thy mess is willing to be killed.'

And – 'this is my Body … Take, eat.' Walk on: be patient, trust – which in Latin is etymologically connected to the word we translate as 'faith'. I can't expect to understand all mysteries. The remains of the bird also remind me that I do have Rosanna's delicious sandwiches in my pack and that breakfast, a poor restrained thing, was some hours ago. I need lunch too.

By this time I have come to Pope's Corner, the confluence of the Old West River and the Cam – nothing to do with the lost pre-Reformation world. In 1850 a man called Richard Pope built a pub here. The Fish and Duck was big: seven rooms and 12 stable blocks, all to cater for the trade on the river, much of which was horse drawn. Now, no pub, just a sprawling marina offering everything from basic chandlery and Calor gas to electricity hook-up and Elsan disposal. Pleasure boats all … But how busy with working craft this river once was, even only a century and a bit ago! I once knew a lot about that trade and its crafts, about (for example) the legendary horse called Captain, around 1900, who pulled the barges and would unbidden leap the ditches and fences as he came to them, knowing to let the barges catch him up a bit to give him slack in the tow rope ... The pubs along the water remember that time. In them the bargees could get a drink and a bed, and oats for the horse that drew the barge, and a warm out of the wind – for working the boats was a tough life. No wonder you learned to swear. The Cutter at Ely by the wharves; the Fish and Duck, where once there was a ferry so you could get over from the other bank; then, at Upware, just by where another ferry – a chain ferry in its last days – used to cross, there was from the 1780s the Black Swan, which after Trafalgar was renamed the Lord Nelson. Its gable end had painted on it, in huge letters, a reassurance to the passing barges: 'Five Miles from Anywhere. No Hurry.' Then came three winding miles to Bottisham Lock, where the Conservators of the Cam take over the management of the river under the provisions of the Act of 1703, and the Sluice at Clayhithe (now called the Bridge), and busy Horningsea, which once was full of pubs. And then came Fen Ditton and its Plough, with its garden reaching down to the river. Now the only passing boats are pleasure craft and the racing shells. Then, as the barge entered Cambridge, the chimney of the gasworks and the foundry would be prominent on the skyline as the boats passed the beloved Pike and Eel – that is gone now, a victim given to greed and the profit of expensive houses – and the sixteenth-century Fort St George, once the last pub on the right bank before the wharves on Quayside.

Busy indeed. Almost every house and field from Horningsea to Cambridge has its dock nibbling into the bank, now a nest for pleasure craft or the secrecy of reeds and osiers and coot and heron. The Romans had docks there, too, to serve the pottery which made a black ware found all over East Anglia. Horningsea – its name gives it away, 'Horning's Island' (and Horning may be someone's nickname, 'bastard': I do like that. What is the story?). For here the water, which for the last few miles has hardly noticeably has been getting less and less above the fields, is lower than the land for the first time on this walk.

I run far ahead of myself: one of the problems of writing this sort of thing. I am still not even at Upware. But you can worry too much about the mind idling away from the projected meditation: as Fr Robert says, just gently bring it back into focus. So no matter, be kind to yourself. *Gratia Dei sum id quod sum*. Even the idling mind can trigger unexpected insight.

And my mind does idle. But it keeps coming back to that quotation Bishop West put all over his chantry. 'By grace you have been saved' (as St Paul says in Ephesians 2:8). That's one of the earliest and profoundest insights in the Christian tradition: it's not because you have purged, by will and discipline, all the darkness in you that God accepts you. He takes you, loves you, just as you muckily are. Not by doing something, not by your works, but simply by being. That means you belong. God has taken you in. Everything you are, the darkness and the light, God embraces in a Love that seeks but will never command your love in return: for love that is commanded is not love but slavery. His Gift has already been given.

There is a corollary. By chance I heard on the Web a conversation, which went to the core of the matter, between the novelist Marilynne Robinson and Rowan Williams, on Lady Day 2019, and one sentence stuck: 'The complexity of any human being is so great as to guarantee that she or he is a unique human being. God made only one of you, and it's up to you to find out what that creation is. What did he make? Who are you? What are you capable of?'

By the Grace of God I am what I am.

+ + +

As I walk along I keep coming across little afloat communities, in all sorts and conditions of boats. Some boats are little better than soap dishes with pretensions – hardly boats at all. There are others that in this their old age remember the North Sea and the shallow coasts of Holland – the bluff bows and the lee boards are the giveaway. But they will never go to the old grey widowmaker again. A surprising number are of that lineage, reminding of the entwined history over millennia of the windy flat shores of Holland and Frisia and this part of the world. They are so much more commodious than the narrowboats – like the one on which my old pupil, friend and colleague Simone lived with her husband. Some of my ancestors worked on the narrowboats of Worcestershire and the Staffordshire Knot. But their boats were never like this, with all mod cons in a narrow-shouldered space. On the narrow canalboats of the Midlands they had no room for a double bed, just a hutch behind the cargo. Some of these boats, moored on the washes well away from Cambridge, where the river spreads itself in a wet winter and the cattle graze in summer to the protest of plovers and the grousing of geese, have been there long enough to have gardens. Hens churckle and scratch round feeders.

Birds: duck, of course, but all the way up to Horningsea the river seemed to be full of great crested grebes. I love them, and their elaborate surprised-looking heads that seem to be wearing a prick-eared helmet of feathers. I do wonder, though, what evolutionary advantage that gives them when they are chasing their prey underwater. Unlike shape and colouration, it seems to have nothing to do with display or sexual dimorphism, as with almost all other species, and it seems almost impossible to tell the sexes apart. (Over my lifetime, that has got to be much more of a problem, not just with grebes.) The grebes can, one hopes: and I find a certain magic in seeing their strange courting ritual when each, breast to breast, presents the other with a scrap of weed. She/he is cheap to keep ... would my beloved like some weed? (No, not *that* sort of weed ...) There was a nest in the reeds by the Fish and Duck. I caught a glimpse of it, and either Mummy or Daddy was on it with either Mummy or Daddy patrolling the river — both sexes incubate, making things yet more complicated. The world is charged with wonder, with the glory of God. Everywhere is a theophany. It shines even through the wandering mind.

I do find it so difficult to keep thoughts from wandering into all the things I am interested in, relevant to this day or not. I feel a certain guilt, shame, for this is supposed to be a pilgrimage, not a nature ramble. But by the grace of God I am what I am. Relax. Be. If your cousins the birds capture your attention, be grateful, give thanks for them.

The path takes me through the new nature reserve, an example of our belated attempt to atone for the harm we have done to our world and our fellow creatures. Highland cows munch at me, thoughtfully. (Highland? They could hardly get lower, for bits of their pasture are below sea level.) Then a big surprise: a water buffalo munching the weed that carpeted the water in a dyke. He's a long way from his ancestral home. I sang the Angelus as I came along the droveway to the Five Miles from Anywhere at Upware, (No Hurry), promising myself, and Left Hip (who was meithering), a rest and a marmalade sandwich when I get beyond it – and I have to go beyond and get upwind, for some clot is burning a heap of plastic fertiliser sacks and the smell and smoke is awful, choking.

It's a strange place, this hamlet I know so well. It's clearly shrunk from what it once was, but I doubt it was ever that big. It's at the end of the straight lode, which the Romans were the first to dig, the head of which is virtually in my garden. They had here a substantial barn or store, with stone foundations, behind where the Victorian old school building stands. Upware was one of the last places in the Fens where the men grew their hair long, and walked up the Lode each year at Rogationtide to the annual Reach Fair to get it cut and to enjoy their annual punch-up with the men of Reach. Once, in the 1860s and 70s, the pub was home to the Upware Republic, a disreputable society of indolent and muscular Cambridge undergraduates who sculled down river for binges of drinking, fighting, fishing, shooting and, in a good winter, the grace of skating. A certain Richard Fielder, a MA of Jesus College, took up residence at the inn, and called himself King of Upware and dominated the Republic and the countryside around with his fists and his scathing tongue. He would fight anyone, bargee or gentleman, at any time, usually winning, and pitching them into the river. He was of good family and high ability, but incurably lazy. His family gave him an allowance to live on, payable provided that he kept away. He it was who originally painted 'Five Miles from Anywhere: No Hurry' on the gable of the inn where he lounged, smoked, drank and fought with the watermen. In the end, apparently, as undergraduates became more serious-minded after University reforms, he retired to Folkestone where he lived in some degree of comfort and respectability.

I thought of him as I walked over the lock at the end of Reach Lode – if you know something of the history of a place, it won't go away, the presentness of the past you know of being always insistent. I wondered what really drove him, what lay behind the longhaired, filthy, violent caricature he made of himself. Despair? What the mediaevals would have called *accidia*, Sloth – which is not mere laziness, but something far more deadly – and we might call depression? It's a subtle trap, always ready to spring, and damned hard to get out of. It can take many forms: not least keeping yourself so busy, your mind so noisy, that you can hide from yourself, deflecting the still, small voice into an ever-deferred future. Which is why a long solitary walk can be a risk: you don't know what that slow rhythm and silence might let surface. *Gratia Dei sum id quod sum ... Deus in adiutorium meum intende.*

Most now might know that last sentence from the better sort of Christmas card, which acknowledges through the lens of art the most unspeakable of Mysteries. Once upon a time every peasant would have heard it.

The Washes at Upware, which only a few weeks ago were water to the horizon and loud at nightfall with the calls of duck and geese, are drying fast in this strange, worrying, weeks long, spring drought. (Into my head comes that line from Hopkins' sonnet, 'Thou art indeed just Lord/ If I contend with thee': 'Mine, O thou Lord of life, send my roots rain.' I hear redshank, but can't see them. How they can feed when the usually soft ground is so hard beats me. A few plovers do their aerial ballet as if only for me – not so, of course. There used to be many, many more. There are greylags, alert and graceful, and the vulgar and excitable Canadas. Then I hear the first cuckoo this spring. Delius? (Letter to *The Times?* – but no, that was when it was a civilised paper.) Yes, definitely, at this spot and with that thought, time for a rest. Lefty agrees.

Rest? Some hopes. I had just started my sandwich when I felt something pull on my trouser leg. A mallard. 'How wonderful,' I thought for an instant, 'perhaps the fear of Man is gone.' For I long for the barrier of fear between the species to break down. As it can do, for example, in those curious reciprocal loves with our animals, where two remote worlds of sense and perception meet and touch, as it did with my dear Hector or my daughter's pony Robbie. Like many people I know, I feel the ache of our isolation from the rest of Creation, the sense of loss at not being able to talk to them. The Lion lying down with the Lamb in the Holy Mountain ...

But no, of course. That is not yet. This was an importunate bandit of a drake who had clearly realised that humans could be a source of easy food. He climbed onto my legs, and, one orange foot on each, marched straight up to my chest and made a grab for the sandwich. He broke a substantial chunk off, but it dropped into my crotch, whereupon down went his head, and in a moment was happily gobbling it. A curious sensation.

Stuffing what was left of the sandwich into my mouth – spilling more crumbs – I raised the camera, and as I did so he made a grab for it, perhaps 'thinking' it a new and interesting sort of sandwich that humans should not keep to themselves. Hence a very foreshortened photo of a duck. But what goes on in duck's head? Probably a lot more, and in a different way, than our reductive mindset allows.

He was not impressed, tidied up the crumbs, walked all round me to make sure there was nothing else edible, and then waddled off to have a nice refreshing sleep. Some animals are indeed bandits. There was a time on the hills above Buxton, when, having opened the car door while I ate my lunch, a wet sheep tried to get onto my lap and nick my sandwich. I gave it a Rolo – which kept it quiet for quite a time, enough for me to finish lunch.

Lefty complained as I got up and told Right Heel to back him up. I told them to shut up. I passed the duck decoy on the wash just upstream from Upware – just by where a century ago there was a little hamlet. The place is almost deserted now: just one farm. There was a chapel, built by public subscription, people sending tiny amounts of money from far away, some – emigrants from this area? – even from the USA. There was a post office, still operative but with little trade when we came to this part of the world, which old Mrs Stanford ran. Her husband ran a sort of taxi service – when he was not busy. The decoy is now fenced securely with chainlink and barbed wire and notices saying 'private'. It is odd to think that what was one of the many places where duck were taken in their winter thousands for the tables of Cambridge and London is now a sanctuary for them, and for the muddy unloveliness of carp. In the thicket of small willows and hawthorn, the cuckoo calls again. You get plenty of reminders of vicissitude and the ephemerality of things on this sort of walk. Yet do we humans actually *want* permanence, stability? We say we do, but we do go odd ways to get it. And isn't the whole thrust of the Gospel, of the injunctions to Abraham and Moses, 'Get up! Wake up! Here is no abiding city, here is no eternal stay.' Genesis' wise poem tells us that human history starts with a sending forth from Eden, away from the security that is no security because our wills spoiled it.

Then the going became poor, really uncomfortable. (Some sort of metaphor there ... I *was* thinking of the walk, not the Expulsion from Eden, though that is true too.) For a couple of miles the bank had been grazed while the winter mud was deep and doughy, and now this long drought had hardened the hoofprints into sharp, ankle-twisting concrete. Left Hip has something to say about it ... 'You just try it ... this is no place for a respectable hip ...I deserve better. Why did you bring me here? No consideration.'

I passed a house tucked down on the drained fen just behind the river bank, more or less hidden by trees. Unseen children noisily play ... 'I'm not playing!' 'Pick it up Jane!' – and suddenly I am reminded of Augustine, in the *Confessions*, hearing children playing a game in the next garden in Milan, and one seems to say, '*Tolle, lege!*' – 'Pick it up, read it!' – and so he did: the Epistle to the Romans. And the rest is history, as they say. Just before Bottisham Lock, backed by fields where older girls were exercising polo ponies, I took a long rest, and read a couple of chapters of Jane Williams' *The Merciful Humility of God* as I ate my remaining sandwich. (I had not told the mallard I had it.) Hard questions she asks: 'What do you regret?' 'How do you choose your friends?' 'Are there relationships that you wish you could restore, which seem lost for ever?' 'When did you last feel joy?' Tick all that apply ... But also 'Start each morning by hearing God say to you, "You are my beloved."' 'Love bade me welcome, but my soul drew back/ Guilty of dust and sin ...' says George Herbert in that marvellous poem of welcome to the stained traveller. Jane makes one think of the upside-downness of the

Power of God, the power of powerlessness, the challenge of the values of the Lord's teaching to all our power structures and the way we think of ourselves: and our property. Our assumptions do not deserve, or need, any argument to rebut them. That silent challenge the Lord gave Pilate is enough. They fall of their own weight. This is a thought which, once you have had it, won't go away. Nor will Thomas a Kempis' remark, which all academics perhaps ought to heed: 'you won't be asked how many books you have read [or written, I say to myself] – when you get to heaven.'

Wisdom: what is it? Good King Alfred wrote, in (I think) his translation of Gregory's *Cura Pastoralis*, that '*ʒeongum mannum ʒedafenað þæt hie leornien sumne wisdom*' – 'it behoves young people to learn wisdom.' (The Dean of Queens' College had that, written out in his lovely italic script, framed on his mantelpiece for all undergraduates to read, mark, learn and inwardly digest. At least they would remember the injunction …)

The Bible puts Eternal Wisdom at the heart of Creation, the Logos (Wisdom 8) – and that passage is clearly related to St John's recognition of Jesus as the Logos made flesh. Even in our common sense, Wisdom is clearly not just intelligence, knowledge of facts or information, for I have known many who ticked those boxes and were foolish. Each of them is admirable but, so to speak, endstopped: its line is separate from others in the poem. Someone – I can't remember who – put it beautifully: Wisdom is synthesis rather than analysis, paradoxical rather than linear, more a dance than a march. It accepts that contraries may both be true. Rational 'knowing' is not enough, as Michael Polanyi pointed out. True knowing is an engaging of all we are with the known. Our intellect, our will, our senses, our emotions, are all excellent ways of knowing in their own kind and with their own limits. But in true knowing they are all involved symphonically. (Isn't it interesting how often Jesus *touched* people? Their senses mattered as well as their mind and emotions. Isn't it true that a friend's touch of sympathy on your arm in time of trouble, or the scent of old incense as you enter a holy place, can do more than any words or reasoning?)

Breaking in on my reading and musing, a friendly yellow Labrador bitch comes running waggily to me and rolls over to have her tummy scratched. Dogs love being touched, just as a horse can go swoony if you rub its shoulder in a slow circular motion – the way its dam would have nuzzled it when it was a foal. I oblige the Lab, and give her a dog biscuit – I always carry a few, just in case I meet friends. But her owner, a hasty, thin-faced woman with a well-practised frown calls her back, 'Naughty dog! Bad dog!' and passes me as if I had not been there. Well, she has her troubles too, which I shall never know. I think a blessing – for what mine are worth – on her and her lovely dog. Time to get moving again.

Lord, with what care hast thou begirt us round!
Parents first season us; then schoolmasters
Deliver us to laws; they send us bound
To rules of reason, holy messengers,
Pulpits and Sundays, sorrow-dogging sin,
Afflictions sorted, anguish of all sizes,
Fine nets and stratagems to catch us in,
Bibles laid open, millions of surprises,
Blessings beforehand, ties of gratefulness,
The sound of glory ringing in our ears,
Without, our shame, within, our consciences,

Angels and grace, eternal hopes and fears.
Yet all these fences and their whole array
One cunning bosom-sin blows quite away.

Herbert: his wisdom has taught me so much, but not yet enough. (If ever?) Bibles laid open, millions of surprises ... I am getting tired, and losing concentration except on putting my feet in front of each other, when, under the unloved A14's bridge, while each heavy vehicle goes over its expansion joint making a thump THUMP that can be heard for a quarter of a mile, in lurid spray paint in among the subway art, 'Jesus saves' stares out at me. 'You are my beloved.' Further along, golden willow catkins strew the ground, curled into the momentary illusion of a conference.

At Clayhithe Lefty and I pass the elaborate little building the Conservators of the Cam built in 1892 to house their meetings and stage elaborate meals out of the (then) huge profits of the tolls they levied for maintaining the busy river and locks, and a few yards further on I find evidence of their still loving care of the traffic. A table of charges for having a boat on the river, a notice that an abandoned dinghy has been found and will be SOLD in one month if not claimed, and then after a hundred yards, a smart notice, just like the signs you see on a road, warning boats there is a weir ahead and to turn back HERE. But on the reverse someone has stuck a printed label just where my eye falls on it: 'Jesus loves you.' With what care thou hast begirt us round ...

We are God's hands in the world. Clothe the naked, feed the hungry, give drink to the thirsty, shelter the homeless, visit the sick, visit the prisoners, bury the dead. Yet that is all very well – these are good actions in themselves, but are they vitiated by being done for the wrong reasons, to make ourselves comfortable? Andrew Marvell, as so often, nudges my memory, turns my comfort upside down:

> When for the thorns with which I long, too long,
> With many a piercing wound,
> My Saviour's head have crowned,
> I seek with garlands to redress that wrong:
> Through every garden, every mead,
> I gather flowers (my fruits are only flowers),
> Dismantling all the fragrant towers
> That once adorned my shepherdess's head.
> And now when I have summed up all my store,
> Thinking (so I myself deceive)
> So rich a chaplet thence to weave
> As never yet the King of Glory wore:
> Alas, I find the serpent old
> That, twining in his speckled breast,
> About the flowers disguised does fold,
> With wreaths of fame and interest.

Why am *I* doing *this* walk? To meet someone? To make a noise? To be, well, *noticed* by those I like and respect? I just don't know if those things are part of the mix of things that made me do this walk, partly, as a way of raising money for homeless women in Cambridge. But should we worry too much about motives? They are a mine field, a mire, are bound to be mixed, and yet the effects may not be that bad. For Alexander Pope, a wise poet, points out that from the excess of the egregious plutocrat Timon, full of civil pride,

> ... the poor are clothed, the hungry fed;
> Health to himself, and to his infants bread,
> The lab'rer bears: what his hard heart denies,
> His charitable vanity supplies.

'Peace, prattler', says George Herbert to his over-busy conscience. Good advice. Whatever we do must be imperfect. Do thou, Lord, make perfect what we make imperfect – as Fr John Byrom used to remind his congregation. *Dei Gratia sum id quod sum.* 'Just as I am, without one plea ...'

The later afternoon is now uncomfortably warm. I did not bring enough water with me, and collapse onto a bench in the garden of the Fort St George with – well, Lent and all that, and I am supposed to be off alcohol, so no pint ... but a pint of shandy is surely venial? It is very, very welcome. I think of nothing, just sit, with my feet up on the opposite bench. I begin to muse about the journey ... walking *away* from Etheldreda's island, through a landscape, which more than any other in what is now called England, has been made in the last 300 years – those three centuries which have seen the abolition of the spiritual in the orthodox, materialist Western mindset. Sometimes it is good to go against the stream.

But pints even of shandy can't last for ever, and I am getting stiff. I get up, stretch, pick up my pack – I knew I would not need that waterproof – slip the straps of my walking poles over my wrists, and head across the Common towards the noise of the town, where I have so many memories. Bunyan's Vanity Fair slips into my mind. I tackle the final trudge on tarmac through the traffic noise, the smell, the crowds of the end-of-working-day town. But, curiously, I notice something has changed: I am walking less hurriedly that is my wont, I am breathing more deeply, I am taking the rhythms of this strange day with me into ordinariness, and looking – well, Thomas Traherne's most famous passage came to my mind unbidden, for 'Eternity was manifest in the light of the day and something infinite behind everything appeared which talked with my Expectation and moved my Desire. The City seemed to stand in Eden, or to be built in Heaven ... The Men! O what venerable and reverend creatures did the aged seem! Immortal Cherubims! And young men glittering and sparkling Angels, and maids strange seraphic pieces of life and beauty.' His eyes let me glimpse, for a moment, the holy in the everyday.[17] That insistent instant passed, but is not forgotten: and in this place of layered memory, where sequential time evaporates, as the signal beeps at me to cross the road by Emmanuel College, there suddenly flicked across my mind a younger me, be-scarved and gowned, in a quieter town, a long ago, still real, world, like a chance whiff of woodsmoke on the breeze recalls every garden bonfire of childhood. Perhaps I ought to be less hard on my memory of my callow, selfish, youth. (Did anyone see *me* as a 'glittering and sparkling Angel'?) Across the road by Pembroke, past a throbbing bus held up in the traffic, and into a Little St Mary's (*recte* St Mary the Less Without Trumpington Gate – I love the old name) quiet, empty, save for the angels. The Cross on the altar is veiled for Holy

[17] Francis of Assisi knew that the finite manifests the infinite, that the physical is the doorway to the spiritual. This principle – call it incarnation is you like – means that Heaven includes earth and earth includes heaven. There are not sacred and profane things, places, and moments, but only sacred things, places, and moments which we have desecrated by our blind selfishness and lack of reverence. It is one sacred universe: we are all a part of it, like it or not.

Week. The end of the journey, the beginning of the next. As I come out to search for something to eat, Emma, once a pupil and now a friend, greets me: 'You made it then? Fr Robert and I were thinking of you, about 1100'. Just when that mallard was mugging me … must be some metaphor there.

I got a chicken and leek pasty at the café by the river. Once the horses, breast high in the water, treading the gravel towpath that runs down the middle of the river, used to draw the full barges up to the King's Mill. I could have eaten another pasty … but no: Mass, and then follow the Stations of the Cross with my even-Christen and Father Gregory. My Beloved arrives from work just in time to be with me. Lefty complains when I genuflect: he never gives up. He is so boring, but I could not do without him. Before each Station we sing a verse of the Stabat Mater in plainsong, then we sing Samuel Crossman's 'My song is Love unknown'. Yes.

6

İSLANDED

Sing to the Lord a new song,
Sing His praise from the end of the earth!
You who go down to the sea, and all that is in it.
You islands, and those who dwell on them.
Isaiah 42:10

You can't walk to islands. Water is the unavoidable threshold that must be crossed by some other means than your feet. This demands making an effort to get there, and perhaps as a result islands have a special place in the Western imagination. We weave myths round them, populate them with dreams, make them a symbolic, simplifying Other for our complicated Normal. The Islands of the Blessed, the Fortunate Isles, Tír na nÓg, Avalon, Hy Brasil, where age and death shall be no more; then there are all the others of more sensuous or material appeal right down to the child's imaginary desert island, to Treasure Island, to the languor of Yeats' Lake Isle of Innisfree, even to Hollywood coral islands and grass skirts swaying to a *hula*. Dante made Purgatory an island on the other side of the world, where the redeemed souls cleanse themselves in joyful suffering to make ready for the feasts of Heaven. In reality, from very early times in several cultures, more than a few islands were special places, sacred places, even truce places when times were quarrelsome: Delos in the Aegean, perhaps Sark, Inis Cealtra in Lough Derg, Lindisfarne, Iona. Disputes to the death were settled by the Icelanders on an island in the Öxará river at Thingvellir at their yearly Althing. Is it by chance that an agreement was reached between King John and his barons on an island? Or that in 1807 Napoleon signed treaties with Prussia and Russia on a raft, an artificial island – which must have taken some constructing – in the Neman river near Tilsit (Sovetsk)? Or that in 1840 the Maori signed a treaty with the British on their sacred island of Waitangi? Crossing to such islands – *any* island – is always, literally and figuratively, liminal. You exchange earth for water, and back again. Things become different. The rules change. You might be changed, as Gonzalo says of Prospero's island in Shakespeare's *The Tempest*: '... and all of us, [found] ourselves when no man was his own.' You can think outside the usual box. Enemies can embrace, as Napoleon did Tsar Alexander.

I share the imaginative pull of islands. I cut my literary teeth on Arthur Ransome' *Swallows and Amazons* books, for like so many children, and especially like many with no siblings and few playmates, I lived in imagination – as one had to do once again in the lockdowns of 2020. I longed to camp on Wild Cat Island, dreamed of having a boat like *Swallow* on the lake, which I had mentally constructed from Ransome's drawings and writing. I wanted to fry a little perch for supper, as Mate Susan did, and so I caught probably uneatable fish in the ponds near our house, but They always made me throw them back. I tried to build a boat out of the thin wood of the boxes in which oranges used to be imported: I had begged it from the indulgent grocer in the village. The dog and I could just about squat in it if I had my arm round him, and in my imagination it was as graceful a craft as ever clove the waves. They would not let me take it to the beach near the house to try it out, though. (Wisely: I think They knew that when I saw it leak it would have destroyed a harmless dream.) Aged eight or nine, I wrote to Ransome, and asked if I could meet John and Susan and Titty and Roger, and where Wild Cat Island was, and I got a charming postcard in reply – which I still have – addressing me as if a friend, telling me that secrets are secrets and should be kept.

I remember finding, years later, on a friend's shelves, R. M. Lockley's *I Know an Island,* which to my shame I have never returned. Much of it describes the life he and his new wife lived on lonely Skokholm, and sheer envy – I had recently got married myself – coloured my reading. My friend Martin – whose book it was (is?) – had spent a year with three colleagues mapping the terrain and exploring the wildlife of Gough Island, remote in the South Atlantic, and I envied him then, and still do. I never did anything like that, but could only dream, play at it, so to speak. After all, to grow old is compulsory, to grow up optional. For example, once, long ago in Coigach in the far northwest of Scotland … the two of us, Jenny and I, took our inelegant inflatable boat out of Achiltibuie to fish, and on an impulse, since the fish did not want to know us, set out for Isle Ristol. Once we got out of the shelter of Tanera Mòr we could feel the longer swells of the Minch lifting the boat. We wanted to feel, again, that special thrill that comes when you step ashore on an 'Uninhabited Island' – a thrill even more acute when you slip over the side of the boat and *swim* ashore to white sand with not even a Friday footprint beneath the fringing palms and manzaneel trees. (Once, in the West Indies, Jenny, now long dead, and I had done just that, and who knows what her dreams were: but that is in another story.) This was very different: Ristol offered a rock-girt little beach of big, rounded pebbles, and behind it blown sand had made miniature dunes with marram grass. We nosed the boat in, taking care to watch underwater for bigger boulders that would damage the propeller. I stepped into the wavelets, and pulled her up. Silence, except for the water. Black dessicated bladder wrack and kelp showed where the highest tides reached, and red runners of silverweed stretched out across the warm sand and shingle into the stones of the storm beach. The low white flowers of scentless mayweed turned their blank gaze to the sun. Our island ... That moment when the bow of a small boat crunches on the sand or shingle, and you jump out to pull her up just a bit more, and the next wave lifts her just a bit and helps you ... to me it is always unforgettable. No matter if within shout there are houses and a road and all the necessary unnecessaries of ordinary life, it is still the moment you dreamed of all those years ago when you imagined *Swallow* as your own. But it is much, much better if the beach is silent, remote, fringed by bushes, or dunes, or if the trees come down to meet where the water reaches – if you can for a moment pretend nobody has found it before you. Once, in Arran, when I was sailing singlehanded I brought the dinghy gently in, dropping the sail at the very last moment, to ground gently on the shingle in a cove near Cuddy Dook. It was utterly quiet, only the rhythm of the wavelets on the stones. Trees and thick undergrowth fringed the inlet. The water was warm on my legs as I got out to pull the boat up a bit. A heron, whom I had not noticed, flew up. He (she?) called out 'Frank', which is not my name, but he has a right to name in his own Paradise. It was the morning of the world, and I was the only man there ... and then, from behind the kindly trees, I heard the school bus change gear for the climb up the hill. You rarely can keep your dream for long: once you got over the little dunes on Ristol you could see where the settlement had been, the fallen walls of black houses where people had been born, lived, loved, died.

Those acted-out daydreams had the advantage (if it is that) of being able to put them down at will. In all of us, I think, there is a niggling desire, instinct (which we can suppress almost totally if we have enough noise in the mind), for a fresh start, a re-calibration, where 'peace comes dropping slow'. But to go for real, permanently, to the harsh isolation of a small island ... few of us have the courage to take that risk, even if we have heard the quiet call. Remoteness, retreat, isolation: abandoning all possessions, going into the desert, to the remote cave high on the lonely mountain – these feature in all the great faiths. There have always been men and women who have chosen such isolation, and who have made, paradoxically, much noise in the world, have become great teachers: the Buddha, some of the Hebrew Prophets. From the Desert Fathers and Mothers, meditating and praying in lives of extreme self-denial in the Scetes desert west of the Nile delta, stems so much of the mystical and monastic traditions – and all the scholarship, philosophy and learning that flowed from them – of the Eastern and Western churches. From the early Irish church's practice of the eremitical life on islands barely habitable or accessible grew so much of what we of Europe in the West take for granted.

Contemplatives, like the ancient Irish monks, are not escaping: they are very far from having an easy time, safely withdrawn from the daily stresses of this world. Indeed, you could argue they do a lot of the hard spiritual work for us. Mystics do a dangerous and strenuous job, like Jacob wrestling with the Angel, who marked him for life in that combat. I have come to think, even with my all too superficial reading of the mystics of the Middle Ages where I have spent so much of my academic life, that they remind us that the boundaries of this life (in our sense) and what is beyond and below and around, interfused with all, are permeable, and that each affects the other. It's not simply a question of knowing, realising, but (I think) coming in however humble a measure to be touched by that Power that moves the sun and other stars. Dante in the *Paradiso* called it love;[18] the Greek of the New Testament calls it δύναμις, *dynamis*, or, as we translate, the Spirit.

I love that idea developed in the Middle Ages of the three interdependent Estates of society – those who work, those who pray, those who defend:[19] each does what the others two do not in (ideally) a cycle of mutual and loving support. There is a monastic community I know, whose members, like many, deliberately 'pray the news' in all its large and small scale awfulness every single day. My friend Mother Cate SSM makes a special point of being up to date with the horrors of The News when she celebrates her morrow Mass each day. It is tough, unremitting, harrowing, work, and without reliance on the Faith's assertion that *through* and *beyond* all tragedy lies the fulfilment of the Promise, it would destroy you, drive you to the cave of Giant Despair. But this is the way the world is: we know that without the travail, danger and pain of birth the

---

[18] '…l'amor che move il sole e l'altre stelle'. (*Paradiso* XXXIII, 145)

[19] It is first fully articulated, as far as I know, in King Alfred's version of Boethius' *De Consolatione Philosophiae*.

infinite possibility of the child is impossible. Risk: it's the name of the game. Moses, Abraham — all that God gave them was a promise. Elijah was given just enough food — no more — for his journey. No guarantees or compensation clauses. But they risked everything. People of faith are the ones who trust the promises will be fulfilled, somehow, and life for them becomes a journey between promise and a fulfilment which may be utterly different to what they had expected. Like all real journeys that matter, it is never a straight line, but always three steps forward and two backward—and the backward step creates, fixes, much of the knowledge and impetus for the forward.

Our culture treats the satisfaction, as immediate as possible, of bodily needs and desires as paramount. It is quite unable to understand what ascesis is about. I have taught students 'about' what I myself could not do — I think I could not do — myself: theory rather than practice. I can only be grateful others can do it, and ask for their prayers. Ascesis is going into training just like an athlete, training the body to work in unison with the mind to apprehend the shadows of the Divine as they appear to mortal sense.[20] So fasting and watching, discipline and silence, were not

[20]   For, so it was held, at the Fall the body/mind harmony was fatally dislocated, and appetite began its despotic rule. Excess of food, far, far beyond what was needed for survival — wholly true in the affluent countries of the world — leads to the unruliness of the desires and the uncontrollable impulses to sex, and anger, and covetousness and sloth. The privation of all that was not absolutely necessary aimed to bring body and desires back into proper subjection to the spirit. Saint Anthony Abbott, perhaps the most influential of the Desert Fathers, said, 'He who wishes to live in solitude in the desert is delivered from three conflicts: hearing, speech, and sight; there is only one conflict for him and that is with fornication.' Another Father, Daniel, said, 'The body prospers in the measure in which the soul is weakened, and the soul prospers in the measure in which the body is weakened.'

ends in themselves. 'Listen' is, after all, an anagram of 'silent'. Far indeed from life-denying, they were a means to achieve a fullness of spirit and to prepare for the Joy beyond the walls of this world which all desire, though they may know it not.

Jesus went alone into the lonely places of Palestine to pray. So, as with the Desert Fathers and Mothers, the spiritual rigour of ascesis, the mystical search for closeness to the Divine was, for the early Irish church, the necessary complement to its daily nuts and bolts ministry among the people. People like Molaise, or Columba, or Columbanus, or Cuthbert, or Herbert, and many others whose names are now no longer on men's lips even though the world we know has been changed by them, sought ever more remote, inhospitable places for their prayers and studies. Even as communities, the Irish monks were pretty solitary, each one in his own little cell – rather like, much later, the austere Carthusians. All round the coasts of Ireland and Scotland and Wales you can find traces of little huts, often ingeniously built of dry stone in places where wood was not to be had. Not much bigger than a large dog kennel, these were the homes of these *athletae Christi*. On Iona one is still pointed out, a circle of fallen stone in about the loneliest spot in the island, where the wind keens in the heather of the moor, and the sound of the restless sea beyond the ancient hill fort to the west underlines the isolation. The roof is long gone. Skellig Michael, off the Kerry shore, a tower of rock rising straight out of the sea with scarce land to feed a hen, was home to a small community. They made little gardens for vegetables out of broken limestone and rotted seaweed and protected them from the Atlantic gales with drystone walls. St Ronan took up his lonely station on North Rona, off the Butt of Lewis, and his sister Brianhuil took herself off to the guano-covered wave-gnawed rock to the west, Sula Sgeir, over which the waves break in big storms. (I went there once, and saw it shining to the west as the dawn sun came above the horizon and lit its whiteness.) She was later found dead in a bothy there, her rib cage sheltering the nest of a shag. People say that sea-lashed Rockall had its hermit; Faeroe certainly did, and when the Norsemen arrived they found the Irish there, who probably brought the sheep, their writing material, that gave the islands their name. Cuthbert, leaving Aidan of Iona's Lindisfarne – 'too comfortable' – meditated for years on the bleak, bird-noisy Farnes. By these standards, Iona with its stretch of rich *machair* was positive luxury, and St Herbert's Island, or Lindisfarne, where Cuthbert was in the end reluctantly constrained to be the bishop, were lands flowing with milk and honey.

The people around these men who turned all normal values upside down gave them huge authority.[21] The folk of Dal Riata and Ulster and the Islands constantly sought judgement and counsel from Columba and his successor Abbots of Iona. Men and women from all over Northumbria constantly bothered Cuthbert for wisdom and guidance; they travelled from all over Strathclyde to seek out wise Molaise sitting in his cave under a rock overhang where a spring has its source in the precipitous west side of Arran's Holy Island. The people of Rheged and what had been Elmet sought out Herbert on his island in Derwentwater for his counsel and teaching.

[21] It is worth pointing out in the Middle Ages the walled-in anchorite or anchoress in a humble church just down the road from you – like the wise lady we call Julian of Norwich – often had great importance and respect in the community, being consulted on all manner of issues and problems. A handbook for anchoresses written in the thirteenth century, the *Ancrene Riwle,* warns them against becoming centres of local news and gossip.

Trips to St Herbert's pretty island are popular – have long been so. When William and Dorothy Wordsworth used to walk over from Grasmere to visit Coleridge in Keswick, the lake islands were about the only places that held mature trees in a landscape largely bare of them (because of the demand for charcoal for smelting the local copper). So they were fashionably 'picturesque', 'romantick', and this one was even more to Romantic tastes as it was complete (once) with hermit. The Wordsworths certainly knew the local tradition that the jumbled stones beneath the trees were what remained of Herbert's cell.[22] Going there led Wordsworth to write a poem (not one of his best, so I resist quoting a poet I revere). Bede – a most readable author – tells how Herbert brought Christianity to this part of pagan Britain (not England yet), how Cuthbert persuaded him to be an anchorite on this island, living on fish from the lake and what vegetables he could grow. (His deep friendship with Cuthbert, whom he visited on Lindisfarne once each year, was the sort of spiritual friendship Ailred of Rievaulx would later have recognised: they prayed to die on the same day, and so they did, in March 687.) But as the rumour grew of Herbert's spirituality and wisdom, people simply would not leave him alone: a hermit's life is rarely quiet and lonely. When he died the Island became a place of pilgrimage for centuries. It still is, each March, for the Roman Catholic parishes around.

The Lakes was – is – very familiar territory to me and my family. There came a year when we took a cottage in summer, in Borrowdale – not Ransome country, of course, but there *were* hills and a lake with islands – and by then I had bought not a

---

[22] The ones we stumble over now are more likely to be ruins of a folly built by Sir Wilfrid Lawson long after Coleridge left Keswick.

larch-planked *Swallow*, but that decent inflatable with an engine. But as soon as you pumped it up and launched it, you realised the unacknowledged lost dream was over: you were not whatever age Captain John had been, but a bit stiff, not so bendable, and the rubber boat was very far from a graceful clinker-built dinghy with a lug sail and the water lapping happily at her forefoot. The noise of the engine ruled out conversation. Nevertheless, she was my boat, a sort of fulfilment of some sort of longing, and we could go to the islands. Years before, on Coniston – which Ransome *did* use – with just my daughter, who was then in the middle of her own Ransome phase, I had rowed splashily out to the island Ransome had called Wild Cat Island. A pilgrimage of a sort ... to her imagination and my memory of my own. She had even said she had spotted the Lighthouse Tree. On Derwentwater, I took the grandchildren out to St Herbert's Island, for my reasons which were not yet theirs. I had told them it had been used as Wild Cat Island in the film of *Swallows and Amazons*. Beatrix Potter based Owl Island in *The Tale of Squirrel Nutkin* on it, as I also told them: another book made utterly unforgettable, this one by the beauty of the illustrations, so that you see the original real through the lens of the imagined. But to the young folk St Herbert's was just an island in Now. It might perhaps stick in their memories, and mature. Things do. But is it not for me to know how, when or why. They weren't especially interested in the overgrown ruins either, or why it was called St Herbert's Island. I would quite like to have told them. The younger grandson, the naval officer to be, was far keener on making off with the boat with that mischievous grin (my mother's grin) on his face, pretending to maroon us: and the girls, to his satisfaction, believed him. No matter: even at that age, he could handle a boat, especially one with an engine. (He's now given up marooning. So far.)

The island was noisy with summer shouts, and other grandfathers or fathers had also read Arthur Ransome, and one family – lucky devils! – had a brown wooden boat called *Swallow II*. Another family had made a fire and were grilling sausages. It was not easy to be quiet, to think of St Herbert, and the hermit's life of prayer and devotion, nor did I then especially wish to, though I dimly guessed I had unfinished business.

+ + +

More recently, I have wondered about spending a night on St Herbert's Island, alone, but it would be hard to do that, for there are many signs that other people do and the last thing I would want is to be surrounded by campfires and conversation. Perhaps I never shall. But my wish to do so, as if something is pulling at me, is intriguing: why do I feel that desire to be less comfortable than usual simply because centuries ago a man chose to live a life of self-denial there? What do I expect? Or seek? Of course, the presence, practice and piety of that remarkable man, made that island a special place, and from it (as with places like Iona or Lérins or Skellig Michael) improbable shockwaves spread out to change the world. The effects of people like Herbert or Columba are demonstrable, undeniable, and I am sure their places never quite forget their having been there, any more than The Helm forgets the people who made the banks and ditches that crown its height. Their resonance is still there, like the way old clothes keep something of the odour and the wear of the men and women who wore them.

There is evidence – there always has been, but we were programmed by our culture not to notice – that this is not mere fantasy.[23] (How badly we need to learn to think outside boxes and off tramlines!) For instance: I was once was in a choir singing Byrd, Tallis and other great renaissance liturgical composers in all that beautifully remains of a late mediaeval Abbey in Dorset. The charismatic choirmaster drove us hard, and he was getting out of us things we did not know we could do. But not well enough. He stopped us. 'You are singing music that could have been heard in this building four and half centuries ago, and the echoes have not died away. Join your voices to theirs. Live up to them.' I began to think – which did not help my singing – of how the Fibonacci sequence – 1, 1, 2, 3, 5, 8, 13, 21, 34, 55 and so on *ad infinitum* – seems to be one mathematical key (very closely linked to the Golden Section, expressed as $(1 + \sqrt{5})/2$, which works out at 1.618033988749894 ...) to so many of the patterns of life, from the complementary right and left spirals on a sunflower head to the harmonies of music to cell multiplication in embryos. Physicist friends tell me that energy is absorbed in the reverse ratio: ... 34, 21, 13, 8, 5, 3, 2, and so on ... it *never* reaches zero, never reaches nothingness. Sound is energy. It's rather like Zeno's paradox of Achilles and the tortoise.[24] But: if the sounds of ecstasy,

[23]   I also mentioned these ideas in *Hungry Heart Roaming*, as I think they are important. If we are going to get out of the parlous mess that the reductive materialist model of the world has got us into, we have got to include the bits that that story, by definition, is not equipped even to recognise.

[24]   They have a race, and Achilles sits in the shade until the tortoise has crawled half the distance, then runs to catch him up, then has a nice snooze again, and then runs... he never, ever, overtakes him.

glory and worship never quite die away, so also do not the shouts of anger, the screams of pain, the Bedlam noise of our quarrels and hatred. J. B. S. Haldane, great scientist but no mystic, once remarked: 'The Universe seems much queerer than we think. Indeed, it may be much queerer than we *can* think.' (*Possible Worlds*, 1927)

+ + +

The first time I went across to Arran's Holy Island – it has the doubled pleasure of being a small island with its own small mountain in a bay of another, already delightful, bigger one with a plurality of much bigger mountains – was in a heavy clinker-built wooden rowing boat that had seen many days. That was years ago, and we went simply because it was an island, it was near the farm where we were staying and its holiness was reduced to its mere name, and we did not even ask why it was so called. Such is youth. The boat's forefoot and keel had a strip of iron so that she could take the odd graze from a rock as she was beached. It was a glimpse of a visit, for Mr MacKenzie the farmer, on whose land we were staying, said he would come back for us in an hour. He said if he left it longer the tide would be running and he would have a hard row back. Perhaps in this world we do get just glimpses of the things that matter, and we don't always know they did till afterwards.

At the landing the lighthouse was just behind us, and beside it were a couple of solidly built white houses for the keepers of the island's two lights that guided ships up the Firth of Clyde. A high wall enclosed a substantial garden, largely given over (apart from an enclosure for hens) to vegetables, which luxuriated in the wind shelter of the high wall and openness to the south. I got talking to one of the keepers, a man a few years older than me. He had his wife and two children with him. I have never met a man more contented with his lot. He had a house, a good job, he and his wife loved the island and its quiet, he caught fish, and in spring he took some gulls' eggs as people had done for ever and a day. He grew vegetables, he had his books. 'What about the children?' I asked. 'They love it. Their friends love coming to stay. They can be free here.' 'School?' 'I just boat them across to the point, and they walk up the lane and catch the school bus. It's only half a mile. Just occasionally in a big southerly or northerly blow I don't do it, but most days it is fine.' He made it sound so easy, so happy. I envied him. I do not know what happened to that contented man when his job disappeared. There will be no more after him, for the lighthouse is now automatic, and no children now make the garth ring with their play.

Many years and much reading, travelling, and much, much questioning later, a return to an island of quite different expectation, with the inflatable and its noisy engine. I cut it as the clear water showed the rounded stones shelving steeply under us, and we glided silently to shore, to a pneumatic bump on a rounded bit of granite. Holy Island: it was utter quiet, save for the swash of the water on the beach and, far off, a gull's cry. The crossing of the water from Lamlash was a massive punctuation mark. Why had we come? Well, it was a small island, and that had been and still was good enough reason, after all. And it really was almost uninhabited apart from the small Tibetan Buddhist monastery near where we landed. It also had a really good hill to climb, even if it is of modest height, from which you could look out over the old kingdoms of Dal Riata and Strathclyde and see the ferry from Ardrossan cutting its straight white wake across the waters which centuries ago the black tarred *drakkar* of the Norsemen had ploughed. Under the waters darker things made their secret way from their nest in Holy Loch. But like so many before us, we had come because once the hermit Molaise, had made it, well, special. It may be it was already a special place before he went there, for the earliest name recorded is Inis Shroin, old Gaelic for 'Island of the Water Spirit.' Places do not have to be Christian to be holy, or numinous, places of power – 'portals', some like to call them. Islands set in strategic places, in the middle of archipelagos or firths, easily accessible from many points, often seem to have been seen so: liminal places, where the walls of the world seem more like curtains. Expect the unexpected.

Of Molios or Molaise not much is known. We never do about a lot of those saints, especially the Irish ones, for Saints' Lives as a genre are never very interested in the facts of biography. They are much more concerned with the grace of God shown through the life, works and sometimes improbably fantastic miracles of the man or woman. He was probably born between 560 and around 570 – just when Columba made his momentous journey to Iona, and like Columba, he was likely to have been of noble family: some say he was son of Cairell, king of part of what is now Ulster, and a Scots princess. Many Irish saints were indeed of high kindred. His legend speaks of miracles from his childhood: such legends usually do. Eventually, he became abbot of Leighlin, in Leinster, visited Rome twice, and became bishop and Apostolic Legate to the church in Ireland. He died in 640. But what really mattered is that, around 20, he rejected the life of a prince and power and chose to retire as a hermit to Holy Island.

There is a path to the hermitage, which many feet have trodden over many centuries, along the shore from the place where you can draw your boat up out of reach of the tide after the passage across the water that sunders the holy place from everyday. But we had chosen not that easy mile by the water, but a harder route over the top and down to the south end of the island. So we followed the line of white stupas over the level fields of the raised beach, up past the well-set farmhouse that is now the monastery and retreat house, and then struck uphill through the young woodland that is gradually bringing to maturity the rare whitebeams (*Sorbus arranensis*) indigenous to Arran, and other native species. Since that first visit long, long ago much of the toxic wasteland of rhododendrons and bracken – Victorian plantings – has been cleared, as if a cloud has been lifted from the grateful land. The pull up to Mullach Beag – the English 'Little Top' doesn't have the same ring – is steep enough and it's only when you have done it that you get a clear sight of what you still have to climb, the rock of Big Top, Mullach Mor. It's a trachyte sill heavily eroded by the huge glacier pouring down, icefall after icefall, from where it gouged out Loch Lomond, Loch Long, Holy Loch, the Firth of Clyde. Once, when the glaciers had already begun to relax their cold grip, Mullach Mor would have been a nunatak standing blackly up from the slow flow of ice on its way to the distant – and much lower – sea.

On the now open slopes, dropping down to a little saddle, we had a momentary sighting of a few goats, who have been here, people say, for more than 700 years, just getting on with being goats. (The lighthouse keeper I met all those years ago had goats too, for milk.) The slope steepened: rock now underfoot, and places where you needed your hands too. Sweaty, we came out onto the summit in the summer sunshine. Prayer flags draped the trig point. Far over the Firth to the southwest stood the volcanic plug of Ailsa Craig. It is home to thousands of the most glamorous of seabirds, the gannet. (It is also where they quarry the blue hone granite for the very best curling stones.) At night, its light – one white flash every four seconds – answers the two white flashes every 20 seconds of Holy Isle Outer light – just below us as we sat. About a quarter of a mile offshore, there was a cloud of gannets fishing. Their scouts had found a shoal, probably of beautiful, fast mackerel, and miraculously the word had got round. (How? I wish I knew. A puzzle exactly like when you are on a deserted beach and give a lone and apparently indifferent gull a bit of your sandwich, and within minutes you are surrounded by importunate watchers making you feel guilty about every mouthful.)

Many times I have seen a gannet cruise, pause in mid-flight, half close its wings, and then, from sometimes 80 feet up, plummet into the sea like a missile, take a fish many feet down, and in the act of swallowing it surface on the other side of the trawler on which I was then working. The white of the bird shifts to a deepening blue for watching eyes as its dive deepens, and the bubbles of its rapid passing leave a deepening turquoise trail behind it, fainter and fainter until it disappears when the bird begins its return to light and air. And underwater they can pursue their prey: they don't have to be spot on in their aim, though often they are. They have evolved perfectly for this way of living, this diving into the sea at about 60 mph – as fast as a woodpigeon, a fast bird, can fly. Their nostrils have migrated to be inside the mouth – which, incidentally, is why they sensibly fly with beaks slightly open. They have developed air sacs in their face and breasts, under their skin, which act like bubble wrap, cushioning the impact with the water. Their eyes, remarkably for birds, have migrated far enough forward on their face to give them binocular vision, so they can judge distance accurately. (But in time, and they do live a fair time, they go blind with the constant impact.) Gannets fishing is a sight to make your heart stop at its verve and predatory beauty. These birds from Ailsa Craig were cousins many times removed of the ones I had met many years before from the St Kilda colony, when we hauled the trawls on that first trip north, or those I had watched feeding their ugly young on Muckle Flugga in Shetland and at Gjesvaer up by the North Cape. To see them rolled up those happy memories with the wind and sun and dancing sea of this perfect day. Strange how beautiful carnage can be ...

'We can't sit here all day', she said, and indeed the sandwiches were finished, our sweat had cooled, and there was hint of a chill in the wind. The descent of the southern side is a good deal steeper, and a bit awkward in bits, as it would be on the downstream side of an ice-plucked hill. One would not be wise to hurry down the broken loose rock. As you drop below the rock boss to slightly more level ground, suddenly, at your feet, running along the grain of the hill, is a chasm, not too wide to step or jump across, but half hidden by plants, and in places deep down to where the sun's light is faint. The trachyte had cooled, and split apart in some shrugging of Gaia in her sleep, and at the bottom my torch beam showed what looked like bones. How old? Who knows. Once this island had been farmed and old (how old?) drystone dykes on the lower bits showed where the in-bye land had been. But sheep would have been run on the hill, and they could well have fallen in. Or perhaps it had been one of the hardy little dark Soay sheep who have been introduced to the island. The bones did not look big enough for one of the ponies.

It was just as we came to the end of the cleft that we saw them: a few Eriskay ponies, mares, with a couple of half-grown foals. The Eriskay breed are the last survivors of the original native breed of Scotland: their blood line reaches back to the ancient Celtic and Norse breeds. Introduced to the island some years after that first visit of mine a few decades ago, they have done well: their dense coat is tough enough for any weather, they find grazing enough and, with the clearing of bracken, more of it, and richer, on the high shoulders of the hills, or here, on the softer ground at the south end. They could not have cared less about us intruders. They are quite wild, and find their own balance in how they live together. Over the years, after a period of unrest and fighting, they now have sorted themselves into three groups: one with the dominant stallion with his harem of mares and his foals, another older group with a dominant mare, and a small group of young animals, who, as they get older, will get restive and seek dominant positions themselves. They'll sort it out.

We dropped down through where the gulls had been – the same place as when I first came decades ago. Most had now fledged, and only a few late ones still had young to feed. The smell of the gullery was less than it would have been a few weeks earlier. We crossed the dyke that marks the in-bye land, and into the green turf of what had been once a little farm. The tight grass, a bright green after the subtler hues of the hill, had a springiness to our tread as if it remembered the long ago nibbling of sheep. Just up the hill from the no-nonsense white solidity of the old lighthouse keepers' house, built by the Stephenson firm, the abbot's house reminded of other hills half way across the world where rhododendrons were native.

The path along the shore was easy, quiet going, contemplative, walking that did not demand conversation. At intervals, signs of the Buddhist presence reminded us that the holy has many names and ways of calling to you. On rocks large bright paintings of the Buddha, of Marpa Lotsawa – Marpa the Translator – and of the Green Tara, surprised at corners: painted texts enigmatically proclaimed their wisdom to the creatures of the sea and air.

We came to the hermitage. Once upon a time a drystone wall closed up much of the cave mouth, Molaise's cell and his oratory, against the weather. There are carvings on the walls, just simple crosses, perhaps made by pilgrims – Heaven knows when. There is a clear spring nearby, still called the Well of Healing, and in 1769 Thomas Pennant's *A Tour in Scotland* records that 'the natives [the ideological implications of that word!] used to drink and bath in [the well] for all lingering ailments'. He describes the water as 'gushing out of a rock', which it does not exactly do now, and you could only wash your feet rather than bathe in it. But it is still cold and clear. Between cave and spring stands a large level stone. A step, and seats, are cut into it. Here, on this Judgement Stone, or St Molaise's Table, legend plausibly has it he would hear disputes and give counsel.

Some runes carved into the rock name later Norse visitors, Christian by then, no longer regarding monasteries as easy meat and monks as fit only for slavery or slaughter. I traced one inscription with my finger, wishing I had memorised the futhorc better: 'Vigleikr the Marshal carved'. We know him: he was one of Haakon of Norway's men, who came with the Great Fleet in 1263 to assert Norway's claim to the Western Isles. They sheltered in Lamlash Bay, just behind me, before giving battle to Alexander III's men at Largs. A stalemate: and Haakon's death in Orkney soon after marked the end of Norwegian power in the west. Those runes suddenly bring that moment very present: what was Vigleikr thinking as he laboriously carved his name in the ancient holy place on the eve of the battle in which he might fall?

There was a ladle, on a chain, by the spring. I drank of the good water, cold, clear, as the saint would have done. I have no idea whether it met current EU standards for potable water.

Then: round the next buttress of the hill, a sight I never want to see again, which almost broke my heart with powerless pity. From far, far above, a half-grown foal had tumbled and bounced – it makes you sick to think of it – down the cliff. It was horribly injured, and still just alive, lying a few feet from the sea. How do you put a big animal like that out of its pain with only a Swiss Army knife? You don't even try. You leg it as fast as you can to the landing, you get the monastery to ring across to Lamlash for a vet, who – most reluctantly – did agree to come, an hour of what must have been agonising pain or so later. You go away sobered, sharply reminded that terrible suffering and the obscene shadow of death, the lot of all that is, never goes away even if, on the brightest of days when nature's smile seems for always, you have been able to forget it. The perfect beauty of the gannets' dive that so delights me is not enjoyed by the mackerel. Last winter, on a lovely frosty morning, when as I left the house I rejoiced to be alive, I saw a sparrowhawk, a beautiful bird, tearing a live blackbird apart. I have seen the ichneumon larva eating its way through the living caterpillar that will never now be a summer butterfly. I think of seeing a grieving Humpback whale holding on to her calf, dead and rotting; of a seal pup, stranded on a gorgeous Norfolk beach, just alive, with its eyes being pecked out by the beautiful beaks of the dapperly plumed gulls. I think of the animals and insects poisoned by our clever chemicals, of what humans have *chosen* to do to hens in a commercial chicken farm, of the beating of the burdened ass falling down under its monstrous load. I think of men and women, some in my wife's own family, herded into gas chambers by men who were reassured by those in power that they were doing a good and righteous job. I think of a man despised, rejected, naked, nailed to a cross as people in holiday mood jeer at his suffering, I think of the innocent flies feeding on his blood on that lovely, sunny spring morning when the winter was past and over and the time of the singing of birds was come.

Our culture – our human mindset – so much wants to see things as all good or all bad. But our everyday experience in these shadowlands ought to have taught us that all power is tainted and taints in its turn, that there are no perfect structures, no perfect people. The shadow side is as real as the other – and it is very easy to see how emotionally that could pull you toward Manichaeism. All of us, it seems, are trying to avoid facing the mystery of suffering, death, and resurrection being somehow complementary to each other, instead of learning how to carry the burden of that knowledge patiently, as Jesus does, who is both crucified and resurrected at the same time. In the terrible beauty of a volcanic eruption, in the elegant Fibonacci curve of the breaking wave of the tsunami, in the deepest sufferings of the world, there God is too. For he has suffered himself, deserted, despised, destroyed by those who knew not what they did, God suffering fully as man in the suffering world in an eternal Now.

Without unmaking there can be no making. Without the death of a star there can be no new worlds. Without the fall of the leaf there can be no spring.

7

FORTUNATE ISLE

An I mo chridhe, I mo ghraidh:
'Iona that is my heart's desire, Iona that is my love.'
St Columba

Iona has drawn – draws – all sorts of people. About the same period as that first Holy Island visit, many years ago, it drew a perverse and foolish me, in my salad days, when I was green in judgement (oh how true!), cold in blood – you could even say, not yet awake. I then knew nothing of Columba, and the insistent, shy rumour of the holy my mind was too noisy to recognise. Iona was just another small island, and I already liked islands, and my cousin David had said he had enjoyed going ...

But that visit – a day trip from our camp on Mull and a day of rest from big walks on the hills – has left small memory: I can remember sharply water as clear as gin – quite unlike the sandy opacity of the sea beside which I was brought up – by the quay as we waited for the ferry at Fionnphort. I can recall looking down into its magic, seeing sea urchins slowly grazing on the algae, anemones' tentacles waving like a *corps de ballet* in the endless search for food. I have a memory of a plume of spray shooting up high from a blowhole at the back of a sea cave as the stiff wind piled up the waves, behind which was nothing till America; of sandwiches eaten by the western beach, sitting on the edge of the machair. Nothing else. I don't even remember going to the Cathedral, or noticing the Norman ruins of the nunnery. Yet I must have seen them. Just as I have come to realise that books need to be re-read and music to be re-heard many times, so I have come to realise that the experience of place needs to be revisited, either actually or through the alchemy of memory as you become *able* to see. I think you grow into being *able* to know or understand things – or some people do. Experience bears out that remark of St Thomas Aquinas (who anticipated so much of modern Critical Theory!), *quicquid recipitur ad modum recipientis recipitur* – 'whatever is received is received according to the receiver.'

For the me I was then, the island was utterly unremarkable. Physically it still is. Take out the Cathedral site, and there is not a lot to draw the visitor. The island is small. Its cliff scenery is pretty average. Its highest hill is about 350 feet – about two thirds of Blackpool Tower. Its sea fishing (one of my old passions) is difficult, its services barely adequate. Arran's Holy Island has it beat on all save the last count. And even if you do count in the cathedral and nunnery, there are many Norman buildings much nearer home that are far more interesting: the architecture here is pretty run of the mill, and much is 1930s reconstruction. Yet now, many years and much experience later, and the growth of – well, longing for that which I cannot name – I see the place quite, quite differently … It is one of those places where the walls of our world seem more like frontiers of knowing, seeing, seem permeable – *if* you can let go, *if* you can let be. (I think, sometimes, we – I – try too hard in our spiritual practice, and ought simply to shut up and be quiet, and listen. Hard.) Iona is important, a sort of node where many ways of being come together, and has long been thought of as that. Adomnán, ninth abbot after Columba, tells how Columba went alone one day to the machair by the Camas Cuil an t-Saimh (The Bay at the Back of the Ocean), straitly charging that no-one should follow him. But one of the monks obeyed him only by the letter: he went by a different route so that he could watch from a hill – probably (for I have tried to work out his possible route) Cnoc nam Bradhan, 'the Hillock of the Brow', where the rough ground and sour grasses of the moor fall away to the sweet turf of the machair. At the edge of the machair there is a rocky outcrop, still called in the Gaelic Cnoc nan Aingel, the Knoll of the Angels. It is a *sidhean*, the sort of place where the old wisdom says there is a passage to the Other World, the world of the Sidhe.[25] There stood Columba, and the disobedient monk saw him conversing with beings too bright to look at: with angels, he said.

Well, take it at face value. Try the thought experiment: what must it be like to talk to Angels, beings of such power and glory? Why in the religions of Antiquity is there such a stress on terror, on panic – the very word comes from the name of the god Pan? A

---

[25] To call the *Sidhe* 'Fairies', with the modern connotations of that word, is gross misunderstanding: in ancient legend, common throughout Europe, especially on the margins, they are powerful beings who can be dangerous, but are not malevolent. They inhabit the same Creation as ourselves but in a different mode. How ancient these stories are is a problem: some of the Irish stories connected with Cúchulainn reflect a society unlike any of which we have knowledge and some scholars think they may in part go back to the Bronze Age. The utter unknowableness of how you *thought* in the past, when the world circled a different sun seen with different eyes, again…

story by John Buchan, *The Wind on the Portico* (1928), memorably imagines what a real encounter with the supernatural, with Phoebus Apollo himself, might be like, no longer chastely white[26] and tamed in static marble, or playing around with assorted nymphs in witty verse, but in his full power, fierce and dangerous as the sun at noon. Why should we think that the ministers of God should be any less awesome?

'Beings too bright to look at', the monk said. 'So in a voice, so in a shapeless flame, / Angels affect us oft, and worshipped be', says John Donne, in 'Air and Angels'. Now for me the existence of angels presents no problems, for if you once come to accept the miracle of existence,[27] the plenitude of the little bit of the cosmos we can know, and the ultimate miracle of Resurrection, you have to accept that the world is more various than we can think or know, that the world our senses can perceive is certainly not the only world: as Louis MacNiece put it in another context entirely, 'World is crazier and more of it than we think, / Incorrigibly plural.'

But what must it be like to talk to such beings, to see them? What was it like for His Mother-to-be when Gabriel's glory shone around? One response can only be terror, even, like Newman's *Gerontius* but without his hope, 'Take me away, and in the lowest deep, there let me be'; or, like His Blessed Mother, awe, acceptance, the proud humility of 'Be it unto me according to thy Word.' For fear, awe, overwhelming reverence, must be

---

[26] Which is quite wrong, for Antique cult statues were painted in garish colours in what I would call the worst possible taste.

[27] Margaret Fuller, who edited the transcendentalist magazine *The Dial*, is reported to have said in 1846 to Thomas Carlyle, 'I accept the Universe!', to which Carlyle replied, 'Gad! she'd better!'

proper before the ministers – angels, as the Greek translates the Hebrew – of God. For nothing about our God is tame, or cuddly, like a teddy bear: the writer of Hebrews knew (10:31) that 'It is a fearful thing to fall into the hands of the living God' for his love makes us know as we are known, which few of us can stand, and makes us what we can be, which few of us dare.

I wonder, was it because Iona had already been a holy island in another faith that Columba made his way there in the first place? Perhaps. We can be certain that this fertile, well-favoured island was not an empty place when the soft leather of his curragh first yielded to the rounded stones of the beach where he landed. That must be true even after the catastrophic decline in population of the previous 100 years – plague, climate change and all that goes with it had led many of the margins of Europe to be emptied of inhabitants. And long before the grey sheen of iron came, people who used tools of bronze and horn had long had a village on the sheltered land by the eastern shore,[28] and who knows how they saw, and made, the place? Was Iona the holy place of which the historian Tacitus preserves a rumour when he records the voyage round Caledonia by the fleet of his father-in-law, the Governor, Gnaeus Iulius Agricola? The vallum, still visible enclosing the monastery, is pretty certainly pre-Christian, and may well have enclosed a *temenos,* a sacred space – which does not exclude a 'fort' of course, any more than it does in Athens' Akropolis. (And I think, again, of The Helm.)[29]

When George MacLeod used the word 'thin' of Iona, he was

[28]   See also what I noted in *Hungry Heart Roaming* (2021).
[29]   Everything inside the sacred space, the *hieron*, belonged to the god. Greeks could find asylum within it under the god's protection, and could not be moved against their will

using a very ancient idea, not unique to Christianity: just as there are times, days, seasons, that can recall us to the sacred so that we can carry something of the insight granted us (in our measure: which may be small) into the everyday, so there are places where many have felt, and feel, we almost cross a threshold into other ways of being, other times. (For me, for example, The Helm, Walsingham, an ugly little church in Norfolk, a chambered cairn in Orkney ... and the cool shadowed vaults of the amphitheatre's walls in Verona dripping fear and howling pain and cruel pleasure ...) What in the Church's calendar are All Saints' Day and All Souls' Day, Candlemas and Easter were already sacred times to the ancient peoples. They were times when the veil between this world and the other was most easily pierced ... when our minds by ritual and custom and community are made most alert and receptive. On these days, in these places, we are granted – if we are ready for it, in the fullness of time, *and* if we open ourselves to accept that we can know what we do not understand – to be aware of deep time, when the tyranny of the linear model of time gives way to past, present, and future time gathered into one. At these times we are reminded that our ancestors are still in us and work with us and through us. The Church calls it the Communion of Saints and we say we believe in it every time we say the Creed. The idea of the Body of Christ, to which St Paul keeps returning, begins in this world – it begins as a metaphor of an actual body, to be sure – but it extends with its risen Lord into the new Heaven, which implies a new Earth in which we no longer live just as ourselves, but in a larger relationship held together by the Holy Spirit.

And why not? The whole pattern of the observable universe seems to be a fullness of self-giving, of constant death and rebirth of stars and plants and all matter, driven by a creativity and energy so great that in the beginning it produced light, gravity, time, space, galaxies, stars, oceans, mountains, valleys, deserts, forests, and us, and our dogs, (and their fleas) and all the other creatures we love, in an infinite variety. And then I try to grasp that this is the great, beautiful, mysterious goodness, wholeness, and aliveness that surrounds us, and upholds us – 'prevent[s] us in all our doings', as Thomas Cranmer's Collect prays. I try to grasp – and sometimes know, in moments as brief as the flashes of sunlight on dappled water – that into this aliveness all of us and all creation will be taken up — in a homecoming, in a reunion, in a celebration, in a marriage where each completed, unique, self finds its journey's end, its butt, the very sea-mark of its utmost sail, the fruition of all its toil. And its – our, your, my – real Name.

Michael Polanyi has a thought – 'Polanyi's Paradox' – that when I came across it went straight to the heart of what I could not then say: 'We believe more than we can prove, and know more than we can say. A knower does not stand apart from the universe, but participates personally within it.'[30] 'Participates personally within it' … necessarily, if that be so, both as agent and as patient. A generation or so ago, nobody had heard of epigenetics. We were fashionably stuck with a rather rigid interpretation of evolution and the determinism of genes. But evolution has not stopped: we are evolving all the time by natural selection – which I regard as one of the most beautiful ideas man has stumbled upon in this mysterious Universe. And now it is widely accepted that a person's experience might alter the cells,

---

[30]   *Science, Faith and Society* (1946).

the DNA (or the way the code is read) and behaviour of their children and grandchildren – alter the evolutionary track, as it were. In fact, isn't this exactly what we would expect if we were to add a little Lamarck to the Darwinian mix? In lab. animals, exposure to stress, cold, or high-fat diets has been shown to trigger metabolic changes in later generations. Small studies of humans exposed to trauma — among them the children of men and women who survived the Holocaust — suggest subtle biological and mental changes in their children. Some recent research argues that PTSD, for example, can be transmitted from generation to generation.[31] The converse must be true: that joy and love and humility and compassion must also have an epigenetic effect.

The implications are profound, and sobering. What we experience or do, in body, mind or estate, has consequences that reverberate in our descendants. That is a powerful argument against everything from smoking to guzzling fast food to immigration policies that split families. The sins (or sufferings) of the fathers ... what Eamon Duffy once called in a sermon 'the entail of lovelessness', at its worst. It also means that each of us carries *within* us the experience, and the moral choices, of our ancestors as well as inheriting, in the material world around us, the consequences of the myriad upon myriad choices they made. I can't (as if I wanted to!) go hunting dodos: they are no longer in the world, by human action. The

[31] Try, for starters, Zovkic, I., Sweatt, J. 'Epigenetic Mechanisms in Learned Fear: Implications for PTSD'. *Neuropsychopharmacology* 38, 77–93 (2013). https://doi.org/10.1038/npp.2012.79 (accessed 25 March 2021); Daskalakis, N.P., Rijal, C.M., King, C. *et al.* 'Recent Genetics and Epigenetics Approaches to PTSD'. *Current Psychiatry Reports* 20, 30 (2018). https://doi.org/10.1007/s11920-018-0898-7 (accessed 25 March 2021).

ecosystem of which they were a part has a gap for ever it did not have before.

We are the very first generation actually to know that, literally and genetically, we carry in us the lives and choices of our parents, grandparents, and great-grandparents as far back as DNA can trace them – which is pretty far back. It does take a village to create a person. We are individuals, but also social animals, each an integral part of a flock. I am because you are, we are because they were, they will be because we are. Deep time, or the Communion of Saints, means that our goodness is not just our own, nor is our badness just our own.[32] The ancestors are alive in us. Each one of us is a node in a past, present and future, we exist as selves in relationship.[33] No wonder so many today, rootless in a world of catastrophic change, seek comfort in, are captivated by, genealogy and ancestry test kits. I have known people cry and laugh at their newly discovered place in a family tree about which they knew little.

'[We are] the heirs of all the ages ...' What a burden! And what a responsibility! And opportunity ...

+ + +

[32] Some things, material as well as cultural, we inherit but are not personally responsible for – which rather challenges the fashion for self-indulgent chest-beating about what our naughty ancestors did. But our having them makes our moral choice of what to do with or about them very important – a different matter entirely.

[33] I am reminded of how – indeed, this may be where my idea has its genesis – Ernst Mach, the great physicist (1838-1916) whose philosophy of science greatly influenced what became Logical Positivism, and influenced Einstein in his thinking about Relativity, argued that objects (in the classical physical model) exist not as simple givens but in a network of relationships by which they define and are defined.

Rosanna and I have been, the two of us, to Iona several times now. Since that first naïve visit I had not been near the place for decades, had not even thought about it. But it so chanced that, very soon after we were married, I went for a walk with Hector and my Lady, grieving for her father's recent death, across the bleak flatness of the winter Fen behind the house. The conversation turned, and suddenly threw up from her the unexpected remark, *à propos* of nothing, 'I must go to Iona'. Instantly, something inside me said. 'Yes!', and without thought I said, 'We go in October', ignoring, heedless of, the certain pressures of teaching commitments. She said later she did not know what made her say that momentous thing.

So we went, knowing that we were starting something, alone and together, which might be – might *not* be – profound. It was a decision as unconsidered, unexpected, unmotivated, as was that to climb The Helm that day, or to do a solitary walk of mile after mile along one of the old pilgrim routes of mediaeval England. Out of the blue: once made, a sense it was right, even inevitable.

Of course, one does one's homework: reading about the place before and after going seems important, rather like filling in those colouring books for children one used disappointedly to be given by visiting and presumably well-intentioned adults. Colouring in the outline: yes, that is what it is. And of course that makes the next visit, and the next, as well as the memory, richer, for the reading becomes inscribed onto what one physically sees. Iona has become polychrome, polychronic. Columba's community, the raids of the Northmen, the slighting of ten centuries of devotion in the name of Reform, the tourists who came when the middle ages and monks and hermits became fashionably 'Romantick', the formal revival of the island as a place of prayer and meditation and exploration, and your own memories of being there – all that becomes part of the polyphony as we draw nearer on the next visit, and time becomes a tapestry.

You cannot, for example, forget (once you know it) that that this little place was once one of immense political importance. Whatever the case about Iona as what some call a Portal, Columba's spiritual authority and political clout among the rulers of neighbouring Dal Riata, Strathclyde, Ulster, Rheged – his kinsfolk, after all – soon made it a place, a truce place, where people came to settle disputes, find counsel and healing, and the rapidly growing monastery quickly became a centre of scholarship where nobles would send their sons to be educated. Success breeds success: Columba's relics drew pilgrims in increasing numbers, and Adomnán's *Life of St Columba* (written c. 697) made Iona internationally famous. In this quiet place, where I have heard remarks on the last ferry of the day back to Mull like, 'Oh there's not much there, we shan't go again' (which a younger me could, smilingly and dismissively, have made), many things we take for granted first happened, things which were revolutionary in their time. For many aspects of Christian practice were still being formed when Columba's monks built their cells. Here Christian graves are first marked with a cross. Here the sacral ordination of kings (at Columba's hand) started, with its assertion of the king's responsibility to God; here started the writing of an annual chronicle, here was written the oldest surviving Irish book, the Cathach psalter (very possibly by Columba himself).[34] Here and in

[34] I think many of us carry in our minds a sort of default image of a great saint, looking clean, tidy, devout, with a soulful expression suited to nineteenth-century stained glass. All you need is the organ music. But all my reading tells me that they were tough, hard operators, good organisers, formidable in argument and dispute and with that authority by which our genius is rebuked

Ireland the spark of scholarship and learning was kept alive when turbulence and invasion and upheaval stalked what was left of the Roman Empire in the west, and from here, it lit fires that came to illuminate all Europe. In the 600s there survive more sacred texts and books from Iona than from any other house in Europe. And, also, it was in Iona that laws were first framed to protect non-combatants in war. In other ages those laws have been too often honoured more in the breach than the observance, alas, but that moral perspective did exist. Now, in our age, it simply seems so quaint, doesn't it, to most of our rulers and governors when our weapons are premised on mass destruction not only of humankind but of every living thing within their range.

as 'tis said Mark Antony's was by Caesar. Most of the pictures I have seen of Columba show a wishy washy, almost androgynous, figure. This must be a long way from the truth. Founding and then ruling a monastery is not for cissies. The story is long enough, but worth telling.

St Finnian of Magh Bile (Moville, in Co. Down) brought back to Ireland the first copy of St Jerome's Vulgate Latin translation of the scriptures, and his most distinguished pupil, Columba, made a copy of the Psalter, which still exists – the Cathach Psalter (the name means 'Battler' and for centuries it was carried by the O'Donnells – who came to own it – thrice widdershins around the field of battle, as a talisman.) Finnian claimed that Columba had no right to his copy, that it belonged to him, and in what must be seen as the first copyright case in history, the dispute was taken before the King, Diarmait Mac Cerbhaill, for judgment. Famously, that was 'To every cow belongs her calf, therefore to every book belongs its copy'. Columba, a prince of the powerful Northern O'Neills, refused to accept this arbitration, and the quarrel came to a head at the battle of Cúl Dreimne in 561, where King Diarmait was defeated and some 3000 men slain. Some authorities claim that Columba, monk turned warrior, was banished from Ireland under an injunction to convert 3000 souls to make up for the 3000 men slain in the battle he had caused. Hence the journey to Iona in the curragh with 12 companions, to an island where he could not even see Ireland. Modern copyright cases – the first Copyright Act is 1710 – are rarely so extreme in their consequences.

The long mediaeval centuries culminated here in the cataclysm of the Scottish Reformation. Iona was of course suppressed. Its buildings were destroyed, its pilgrimage dismissed as a mere superstition that demanded eradication and suppression. (For the rumour of the Other, and people enjoying themselves in unpredictable ways – pilgrimages were holi-days, after all – make Authority deeply uneasy). Yet it still held some symbolic importance which nobody could quite forget. For it was in Iona where many kings (including Kenneth MacAlpin, and Macbeth, and Duncan) had been buried for centuries. It was thither, in 1609, James VI had Andrew Knox, Bishop of the Isles, summon the clan chiefs of the Isles and the Highlands to force them to sign the draconian Band and Statutes of Iona.[35] Nine of them did so; what they signed outlawed the Gaelic (which James' grandfather and great-grandfather had spoken fluently), required them regularly to report to Edinburgh to answer for their actions, and to support Protestant ministers in their mainly Catholic lands. It also forced men with 'thriescore kye' (60 cattle) or more, to send at least the eldest son, or, failing sons, the eldest daughter, to some school in the Lowlands, there to be kept 'until they may be found sufficiently able to speak, read and write English.' Thus was the bond that had bound the clan chief to even the humblest of his kin as protector and good lord from times forgotten given the first of its death blows, harbinger

---

[35] It was all part of that attempt to extend royal control, and revenue, which had borne grim fruit when James authorised the Gentleman Adventurers of Fife to 'civilise' the 'most barbarous Isle of Lewis' in 1598. He wrote that the colonists were to act 'not by agreement' with the local inhabitants, but 'by extirpation of thame.' (Somehow, the Latin, which means 'uprooting', shocks less than the Greek 'genocide.' They mean the same.) Blood was shed: and the Gael, heir of proud traditions, became the 'savage' the 'primitive.'

of the bloody butchery after Culloden and the obscenity of the Clearances. Sometimes the voices in the wind have not comfort.

+ + +

Tourists came. (What does that word mean, exactly?) They saw the ruins, they visited the bay where Columba landed, admired (a new fashion) the wildness of the landscape and sea, talked to the locals. Richard Pocock, Bishop of Meath, in a letter of September 1760 in his MS *Tours in Scotland, 1747, 1750, 1760,* told how he

> 'went to the South west part of the Island and in half a mile passed by a fine small green hill, called Angel Hill, where they bring their Horses on the day of St. Michael and All Angels, and run races round it; it is probable this custom took its rise from bringing the Cattle at that season to be blessed, as they do now at Rome on a certain day of the year.'

How curious that that hill where Columba conversed with those bright beings should, twelve hundred years later, have still been venerated as somehow sacred! Later authors, like Thomas Pennant, *A Tour in Scotland 1769* (1771) repeated the story and found parallels elsewhere, for this is the very period when an Enlightenment interest in what we might call folklore as well as the past *qua* past was developing, and when the fashion for things 'mediaeval' was fast growing. By the time Queen Victoria and her beloved Albert came to Iona on their cruise in August 1847, the Highlands and Islands had become Romantic. They had just been to nearby Fingal's Cave on Staffa, about which Sir Joseph Banks had been influentially rhapsodic. I do not know why Victoria and Albert came. Albert, that hugely intelligent and serious Prince, would have done his homework and known what he was looking at when he landed. But Victoria clearly had little knowledge or interest beyond the Romantic imagining of the Highlands as 'picturesque' – that eighteenth-century neologism reminds us of how little that taste could have accommodated Highland midges (especially when wearing the newly fashionable kilt), sheep ticks and bogs. She did not go ashore, but stayed on board sketching while Prince Albert and Karl, Fürst zu Leiningen (her half-brother) went to look at 'the ruins of St Oran's Cathedral' [*sic*]: 'When Albert and Charles returned, they said the ruins were very curious, there had been two monasteries there, and fine old crosses and tombs of ancient kings were still to be seen. I must see it some other time.' If there is another time (There wasn't ...) Just like so many cruise passengers nowadays.

Before her, Wordsworth had come, and Walter Scott. All were pilgrims – they might have refused the word, though – to a place where, 1200 years before, that curragh with thirteen people in it had come ashore and changed the world. My habit of reading up about places makes me sometimes an annoyingly informative companion – or indeed writer – as I ruefully admit, and I have to admit that seeing through other people's eyes and speaking with their tongue really is sometimes a shying away from something you have found powerful, even overwhelming, something that you are not quite ready to acknowledge. Sometimes. But more often it is a feeling of company across the years, fellowship with the company of the dead whom I count as friends, as real. For some reason I love knowing that Samuel

Johnson (whom I like and respect very much indeed, even when he is at his most polysyllabically judicious and rhetorically authoritative) and James Boswell and The M'lean went to Iona in 1771 and slept (very well) on fresh hay in a barn, with their portmanteaux as their pillows. And the Doctor said one of the profoundest things about the way knowledge of the past of a place sharpens the present experience. Boswell quotes his 'great and pious friend,

> ... who was no less affected by [Iona] than I was; and who has described the impressions it should make on the mind, with such strength of thought, and energy of language, that I shall quote his words, as conveying my own sensations much more forcibly than I am capable of doing:

> "At last we came to Icolmkill, but found no convenience for landing. Our boat could not be forced very near the dry ground, and our Highlanders carried us over the water. [Brave Highlander! Giving Johnson's weight a piggyback while wading was heroic.]

> "We are now treading that illustrious island, which was once the luminary of the Caledonian regions, whence savage clans and roving barbarians derived the benefits of knowledge, and the blessings of Religion. To abstract the mind from all local emotion would be impossible, if it were endeavoured, and would be foolish if it were possible. Whatever withdraws us from the power of our senses, whatever makes the past, the distant, or the future, predominate over the present, advances us in the dignity of thinking beings. Far from

me, and from my friends, be such frigid philosophy as may conduct us indifferent and unmoved over any ground which has been dignified by wisdom, bravery or virtue. That man is little to be envied, whose patriotism would not gain force upon the plain of Marathon, or whose piety would not grow warmer among the ruins of Iona!'"[36]

Both Boswell and Johnson were pretty sharp, and diligent, in observing the 'remains of antiquity at this place, accompanied by an illiterate fellow, as cicerone, who called himself a descendant of a cousin of *Saint Columba*, the founder of the religious establishment here.'

Johnson was, as Boswell said, a deeply pious man, whose Prayers are often of great spiritual depth. That's not a trait we associate with worldly, womanising Boswell, but this strange island did elicit these thoughts, which he was happy to make public:

I left [Dr Johnson] and Sir Allan [M'Lean] to breakfast in our barn, and stole back again to the cathedral, to indulge in solitude and devout meditation. While contemplating the venerable ruins, I reflected with much satisfaction, that the solemn scenes of piety never lose their sanctity and influence, though the cares

[36] Boswell has a footnote (this is the first time I have quoted a footnote in a footnote!): 'Footnote: Had our tour produced nothing else but this sublime passage, the world must have acknowledged that it was not made in vain. The present respectable President of the Royal Society [Sir Joseph Banks] was so much struck on reading it, that he clasped his hands together, and remained for some time in an attitude of silent admiration.'

and follies of life may prevent us from visiting them, or may even make us fancy that their effects are only 'as yesterday, when it is past', and never again to be perceived. I hoped, that, ever after having been in this holy place, I should maintain an exemplary conduct. One has a strange propensity to fix upon some point of time from whence a better course of life may begin.

But then ... while the good Doctor was measuring the ruins and recording differences in architectural style, off goes Boswell, just as I would have done, on a borrowed horse to see the sights, over the hill down to 'Portawherry' [Port-na-Curragh], where Columba probably landed, and to note approvingly the fertility of the island, its virtual self-sufficiency and the industriousness of the inhabitants. And that they brew a lot of beer.

+ + +

It is not hard to see why the basalt columns of Staffa were on the early nineteenth-century tourist route, but why this nondescript island too? The rumour of the holy works underground, like a mycelium, fruiting in unexpected places, just as slow, soft, silent mushrooms, ('so many of us', as Sylvia Plath put it) can burst through concrete. The Christian geography of Europe was netted by pilgrim routes to holy sites. It was a geography of stories of the saints and of the riches they had amassed in the Treasury of Grace which could help poor pilgrims trapped in a debt for sins committed which they themselves could never redeem. Men and women of all stations and inclinations had trodden those paths since almost the very earliest Christian times – the earliest pilgrim narrative we have, the *Itinerarium Burdigalense*, recounts a pilgrimage to Jerusalem from Bordeaux in 333 or 334. But where Protestantism allied itself with secular power all that had been destroyed, forbidden. The shrines had been wrecked, pulled down, the bones and relics[37] of saints scattered to the four winds or thrown on the midden – anything of value, of course, being sold: to clear the debt of the Crown, to enrich the parvenu, to buy a jewel for a wanton ambling nymph. But in soil, that infinitely complex powerhouse on which we all depend, you can't ever quite get rid of mycelium: *naturam expellas furca, tamen usque recurret,* 'you can chuck nature out with a pitchfork, but it will soon hurry back', says Horace. Even so with that need for spiritual sustenance at the ground of what it is to be human and conscious, a need for which we have no name.

So Walsingham, Canterbury, Lindisfarne, Glastonbury and many other places never quite lost their hold on the imagination and memory even when what you were remembering them for was indistinct, nebulous, even dismissed as superstitious (the root

---

[37] It's easy to sneer at relics. But we clever moderns have a cult of relics every bit as pervasive as anything the middle ages knew, for it is a natural human need born of love and honour. 'That was my mother's vase, that was...' Diana's dresses draw thousands of visitors; Tolkien's old MA gown made silly money at auction; memorabilia of the Beatles, letters written by the famous, give auctioneers a good living. I plead guilty too, for the lead that our beloved Labradors used still hangs, with a slip collar, on the hook by the back door even though the dogs are a warm memory. Those leads are as much relics as the fragments of bone or cloth to which people made devout and arduous pilgrimage. After the Second Council of Nicaea in 787 it was obligatory that any newly consecrated church should have a relic in its altar. I found a thoughtful essay by Matteo Salonia, 'The Body in Medieval Spirituality: A Rationale for Pilgrimage and the Veneration of Relics', *Interdisciplinary Journal of Research on Religion*, vol. 14 (2018) illuminating on the sort of mindset that our forebears might have had about the sacredness of the body.

meaning of which word in Latin is, ironically, 'survival'). The old shrines, the old relics, are no longer there but their places still draw people. Little by little, foot by tentative footfall, the pilgrims have come back – not in curiosity, or as mere antiquarians – perish the thought! – but as searchers for that which they acknowledge but cannot comprehend or even verbalise. Pilgrims once more flock to Walsingham. They make their way to the shrine of the Black Virgin of Willesden, the parish given to the monks of Westminster by Aþelstan in 938.[38] Even as I write this, I hear of a new/ancient pilgrimage the Reformers thought they had got rid of: St Eanswyð, granddaughter of Aeþelbert of Kent, sister of St Aeþelburӡa, Edwin of Northumbria's holy queen, died (around 650) no older than 22, having refused marriage and founded the first women's convent in England at Folkestone. Her relics, objects of devotion for nine hundred years, were hidden away in a reliquary made of re-used Roman lead in the walls of the twelfth-century Priory church to which they had been translated, and all that was mortal of her slept there until builders found the urn in 1885. Recent osteoarchaeological, C^{14} and DNA analysis has made as sure as ever may be that these are her remains, and already pilgrims, especially from the Orthodox churches of Eastern Europe, are making their way there. But you never recover what the past was, you can't un-be what has been and what has made you: you have to use the past to make a new thing, a new future.

[38] Thomas Cromwell's men dragged the original image to which St Thomas More made his pilgrimage, shortly before he was beheaded by the king he had loved and served well, to Chelsea, where More's home was, and burnt it in 1538. About a century ago – just when Fr Patten was working at Walsingham – the then vicar, James Dixon, restored the shrine, and the pilgrims came. The new statue (by Catharni Stern) was dedicated in 1972.

FORTUNATE ISLE

Like the wintering geese flying in from the far north and the hard work of summer, we return, together yet each for our own reasons, around the Autumn equinox, in the weeks leading up to Samhain, to this holy place. I would give a lot to be able, given the time and the energy (I never used to worry about that), to walk there across the emptiness of Mull, letting the rhythm of walking the rough old road, not everywhere obliterated by modern tarmac, seep into me, slow me down from my customary busy-ness. Such a journey would once have been the usual thing, and along the route standing stones marked it, of which a few still stand. As Johnson and Boswell found when crossing Skye, the ways were tricky and deceptive, and you needed a guide or markers. But we have to make do with the minor punctuation marks between this – pilgrimage, for that it what it has become – and the everyday: boarding the ferry at Oban, then leaving the car and all one cannot carry at Fionnphort to take another ferry across the sound, to the grateful silence of an island virtually without engines.

In another book I have written a lot about Iona, about the people we have met by chance there, about the way the holy intersects (if you let it) with the daily prose of looking after the animals, getting in the hay – all the daily business of running a farm. The holy does not set aside the daily, and the material; it transfigures it, like the sun directly behind the companion with whom you are walking in the mist of early morning makes a glory. (I have wondered, idly, if what the disciples saw and could not properly describe on the mount of the Transfiguration was materially expressed by such a phenomenon.) But if you try to make that transfiguration happen, it won't: it is a gift, a grace.

Perhaps it is because you half consciously expect the unexpected in Iona that you are open to things that are always there, but you often never see: a tiny gilt cross deposited on a pattern of stones in the inch of water running beside the path can be of sudden huge significance; meeting a person coming the other way over the moor, and a silent greeting, a meeting of eyes, a blessing given and received. A woman sharing the table at the retreat house casually, without knowing it, makes a remark that strikes to the heart like a rapier thrust, and nobody notices, and she joins you both for saying Compline overlooking the wind-combed sea: the beginning of a friendship across many time zones. You will probably never see her in person again, only Zoomed. But a tiny part of the chain of love that holds everything together is now stronger. The significance of the insignificant ... too often the noise of everyday can hide it. And how often it is that the concrete, often trivial, thing nudges you into seeing for a moment the Universal. In this bit of ivy-leaved toadflax which the wind is stirring on this stone wall is a glimpse of the universal Flower dancing on the Rock. Which is why in pilgrimage or retreat you try at least to turn the volume down, why mindfulness and memory, and the stillness that may herald prayer, are so important.

The most recent visit was heralded by the first big storm of autumn: it would not be the last as that catastrophic COVID year unwound to its close. We were lucky to get across the sound before the southerly gale butting against the tide closed the ferry. Migrating birds were blown about on the wind, with the geese battling the gusts, webs spread, flight feathers panned, as they came into land. But the ancient rocks of the island, some the oldest on the planet, remained, facing out the noisy passion of the storm in their silent witness.

This was a visit snatched between the lockdowns – hateful word, and the worse when you know its origin! – caused by COVID-19. The familiar, loved, place, was unfamiliarly quiet: the Cathedral, closed; the Bishop's House and Chapel, closed, the Catholic House of Prayer (in the Gaelic, Cnoc a' Chalmain, 'the Hill of the Dove'), our usual roost with its lovely oratory overlooking the dawn sea, closed. Our favourite place for lunchtime soup, run by the Church of Scotland, closed. Good for us, perhaps, for Iona is always a place where you feel you are letting known things go, first as you make your way along that empty road over the Mull hills, where the importunate phone does not work and cattle across the road could not care less about your hurry, then, disencumbered of all your car stands for, walking down the slade to the ferry's lowered bow door grinding on the concrete as the waves lift and lower, lift and lower, as they build up in the strengthening wind and the running tide. Will it be able to dock on the other side? Will it run tomorrow? You have to go, like many thousands before you, just as you are, more or less … There is no guarantee you will get back when you plan to. Let go. Stop. You have no option.

Locked doors. Knock and it shall be opened … Rosanna's favourite spot for meditation, a quiet corner of the Cathedral where people have left little patterns of beach stones, written requests for intercession, a little wooden cross on the windowsill, she could not get to. I could not get into my own favourite spot, the twelfth-century St Michael's Chapel, where a single window on the east lights our darkness in the two rows of stalls. That place will always hold the memory of a late afternoon, a storm beating on the roof and the wind piping now high, now low, through the door, and a wet Hector breathing quietly, asleep at my feet as I sat, silent, facing the Y-tracery of the east window in the dying of the light. That was his last trip to Iona.

Knock and it shall be opened … One morning early … Well before breakfast I went out, into the familiar quietness, the new strangeness of the place, as the dawn brightened behind Ben More. It would rain again soon: in fact, the first sharp shower coming up on the fresh wind soon caught me. It was far too early for the ferry to be bringing the daily tide of folk coming over for the day, for all sorts of different reasons, from the devout to the dump lorry emptying dustbins. I have come to like, selfishly, to have the place to myself. I went along the road to the Abbey, knowing that it would be closed, but saw that the door of St Oran's Chapel was open. Ought it to be? As I went in below the twelfth-century archivolts, a bird flew out just above my head, and I realised that some kind soul had left the door open on purpose. For there was a martin – not a swallow – nesting late – very late indeed, up here! – in the muddy cup high up near the roof. Psalm 84 came to mind yet again: 'Yea, the sparrow hath found her an house …' I love that verse (and that psalm, which is full of love and hope) for what it says about the joyful peacableness of the Lord's house. There is, of course, a smell of bird droppings. It is an old smell, that the old ones would have known as part and parcel of going into the churches where they worshipped year in year out.

The abbey door was firmly locked, as I expected. But, slyly avoiding the notice of three wet people, early birds like myself, who were desultorily, dutifully, depressedly looking at the clearly labelled foundations of what had been the Benedictine monastery – founded long centuries after Columba came here – I tried the worn-shiny latch of the tiny door into the shrine – another of my favourite places, which I do not really like to share – where ten centuries of pilgrims had come to venerate the relics of Columba. To my joy it gave to the hard pressure of my thumb: it was unlocked! I waited, looking innocently interested in something in the grey sky, until the wet people had moved on, and while the going was good pushed at the door. Its foot scraped on the stone. Knock and it shall be opened ... Stooping almost double, I entered the tiny space which has room for about six people. Inside, in the semi darkness, I could make out the Lord's face in the icon copied from that in the monastery of St Catherine on Sinai,[39] and another one of Blessed Mary, Theotokos, a small light in the darkness. Here is where Columba was buried, almost certainly, and when they excavated they found two burial kists of roughly the right date – they had been robbed, of course – in the floor.[40] I shut the door, hoping that others would think it locked. I sat quiet, hearing the rising wind against the roof. Time slowed. A simple altar, the icons, one of Columba with the horse that wept for him as he neared death,[41]

---

[39] One of the few to survive the wholesale iconoclasm in the Eastern Church in the eighth century. St Catherine's icons were safe because the monastery was in the lands conquered from the Greeks by the Muslims and they were relatively tolerant of other People of the Book.

[40] They were almost certainly those of Columba, and possibly Adomnán.

[41] Adomnán, in his 'biography' of the saint, recounts that Columba, now old and weary, set out in a cart to visit the brethren working in the western machair. (You can still see where their lazy beds were.) He said to them, 'I had a great longing, in the high days of the Easter feast, to go to the Lord; and he granted it to me, if I so willed. But I would not have the joy of your feast

and me, just as I was, damp. The wind could hardly be heard. Be still. By the Grace of God you are what you are.

Prayer is awfully hard work sometimes, and you may as well admit it. Sometimes you think, 'Am I fooling myself?', but you stick at it, and that is the point. Plod plod plod. 'My words fly up, my thoughts remain below' – yes, I know what Claudius felt, and I have not got an Old Hamlet on my conscience. (Who am I to judge how grave a sin is?) My mind wanders, and I get so irritated with myself. (But the disciples themselves could not watch one brief hour ...) And sometimes just to give up, to sit quiet and, in the silence and the stillness, to let the mind fall into idling, even the idling of exhaustion – well, that is something, that too is important. I think we – I – talk too much, think we

turned into mourning, and so I willed to put off the day of my going a little longer.' His friend Diarmid was grieved to hear this, and Columba continued, 'Truly is this day my Sabbath, for it is my last day in this toilsome life, when from all weariness of travail I shall take my rest, and at midnight of this Lord's Day, I shall, as Scripture saith, go the way of my fathers. For now my Lord Jesus hath deigned to invite me; and to Him, I say, at this very midnight and at His own desiring, I shall go.'

The Saint set off back to the monastery, and halfway there sat down to rest. And as the Saint sat there, a tired old man taking his rest awhile, up runs a white horse, his faithful servitor that used to carry the milk pails, and coming up to the Saint he leaned his head against his breast and began to mourn, knowing (as I believe) from God Himself – for to God every animal is wise in the instinct his Maker hath given him – that his master was soon to leave him, and that he would see his face no more. And his tears ran down as a man's might into the lap of the Saint. Seeing the horse, Diarmid would have driven him away, but the Saint stopped him: 'Let him be: let this lover of mine shed on my breast the tears of his most bitter weeping. Behold, you, a man with a mind that can reason could in no way have known of my departing without me telling you; yet to this dumb and irrational beast, his Creator in such fashion as pleased Him has revealed that his master is to go from him.' And so saying, he blessed the grieving horse his faithful servant, and it turned again to its way.

know the agenda we ought to be following, so that I/we have forgotten how to listen easily. Anyway, glory and trumpets all the time would not be bearable. But to achieve interior silence is so hard – I know that when I spent that time in that welcoming monastery that was the biggest challenge, and one only partially met. Perhaps I was trying too hard, scolding myself to be silent. But that anything at all was met was a grace: and be not too hard on yourself. *Gratia Dei sum id quod sum.*

My tummy rumbled, reminding me that man is a body, thank God, as well as a mind and a soul. What a joy, how *right* it is, that in the Creed we talk of the Resurrection of the Body! How right the mediaevals were to stress the physicality of heaven, eating and drinking and singing and dancing! For matter is holy: it must be, for God makes lots of it, and without the matter of our bodies we would not be ourselves. The Lord himself went through the messy, undignified, helpless business of birth, and through His Mother shares so much of our DNA. No longer are we merely creatures of a distant God, but cousins. Our very appetites, from steak and kidney pie to claret to sex, are by nature and origin holy. There is no division between the sacred and the profane, only between the sacred and the desecrated. But high thought, even when full of joy, is not proof against tummies rumbling ... Back where we were staying they had promised black pudding.

I got up, pulled the little door open, peered out to see if anyone was about, for I was pretty sure I was not supposed to be there, and came out very carefully into sunlight. But I was too hasty, as ever ... Nobody did see me, but, turning to shut the deeply recessed door, I banged my eyebrow on the stone of the arch, and gave myself a minor black eye. That'll teach you to be selfish and unwelcoming ... I deserved that. It was a good place to say matins before breakfast, and to use the beloved Latin of the Canticles and Psalms where nobody could hear my bad pronunciation except the angels.

They did have black pudding. Of the Scotch variety. It was heavenly.

+ + +

The two of us, as is our wont, had some long slow walks, mostly in silence, including our favourite to the bay where Columba landed in 563. There is a labyrinth of stones, possibly ancient, possibly not, furred by the green turf. We walked it, of course, and at noon sang the Angelus together, Rosanna's alto and my bass in happy unison. We placed a little cairn of beach stones for Hector the Labrador, for this had been one of his happiest beaches. It will last until the gales of winter blow away what we made, but its stones will remain for others to build their own memories. Over the hill, on the machair facing the Atlantic, the rain-washed sheep and cattle munched quietly. On rocks that were old long before the worlds of the ammonites and dinosaurs and trilobites, long before the earliest organic life, here we stand, creatures of a passing but infinitely important moment, understanding their long perspectives just as we number the flaming stars. Those circling stars were as sharp to my old and dimming eyes in that clear air off the sea as they were to my clear but thoughtless sight when I saw them in boyhood from the deck of the trawler on which I was working in the dark of the mid-Atlantic night. Later, we climbed Dun Ì for the wonderful view south to Jura and Islay, and north to Staffa and the hills of

Skye, with the bulk of Mull's Ben More over the wind-combed sound to the east. We took of the water of the Well of Healing just below its summit, (summit? I suppose so, even if only just over 300 feet high) as our friend, Matthew, once my brilliant pupil, had told us was his own custom on his yearly visits.

+ + +

We often walk alone. I had wandered north, past the Abbey with a thought for climbing up Dun Ì again to sit by the Well. But the promised rain was just starting and the wind that had been powerful all night was strengthening, so thought better of it and turned to go back along the shore. By the gate that leads to the shore out of the abbey precincts, there are three concrete steps and a metal post, rusty save for its top, shiny with rain. By it stood the Highland bull – he's a gentle fellow, if a bit short of conversation, whom I have met before – and he was more or less barring my way. For once he was able to see me properly, for his long fringe on his forehead was streamed back by the big wind.

He looked – is – a peaceable soul, chewing the cud, and I opened the gate and – sudden thought – can I learn something from him? – sat down on the steps by him, feeling in the pauses of the wind something of his heat and smell, and, watching him, almost called him Brother Bull who praises the Lord in his way, just by being a bull, like Jeoffry the Cat

> For he is the servant of the Living God duly and daily
> serving him.
> For at the first glance of the glory of God in the East he
> worships in his way.

For he shares the same beginning with me, the atoms in his body come from the same sun that gave, for this brief spell, the atoms that have become me, and somewhere on the genetic tree we share genes. Perhaps I hoped he might teach me something about calmness, placidity, quietness, things I admire but do not have – or have forgotten how to have. The wind stirred the hair over his deep eyes, and picked up and played with the long guard hairs of his coat and tail. Round his neck was a ruff of tight curls, darker than the rest of his russet coat. Occasionally he rubbed his chin, as if thoughtfully, and then his cheekbone, against the post. (So that was why it was so polished.) He lowed gently, looking at me through his fringe: was it a sort of greeting? But perhaps he was scenting the couple of cows in the field to windward of him. Even so, I like to think he was not averse to my company. We sat together for about half an hour. I was sorry when, cud finished, he slowly stirred, gave me a slow, rather hairy, stare, turned away on those huge, splayed hoofs, and started to graze. I got up to go – and remembered that I had the key to room and shelter and had promised Rosanna not to be long. She must be sitting somewhere in the rain without a bull to talk to.

+ + +

In fact, she had managed to get another key, and was quietly looking at the sea through the rain running down the window. We sat in companionable silence for a while – I seemed to be doing that quite a bit that afternoon. 'You ought to take more rest', my Lady often says. She said it again. 'There is no shame in being older than you were.' Ruefully I agree, as I usually do, but as I sat looking through the window at the rain squalls scudding across the sound – it really has become foul out there and I am not as waterproof as my friend the bull – idling thoughts in the stream of consciousness began to eddy round that tough idea of which I can never get the hang – rest. The word nagged at me. Apart from physically lying down, which is often called rest, what *is* rest? Is rest simply a negative, of stopping working, or travelling? Is it what I have been doing this afternoon, thinking at the pace the bull chewed, quietly happy in the small rain? Is it a cup of tea and a piece of cake and your feet up? That might be one pleasure in Heaven, but like casting down your golden crown beside the crystal sea one does feel it might pall. Brother Bull seemed to know when simply to be, and chew things over, and not bother about it. Whereas I fidget.

For the whole of my life has been dominated by work, the ethic of work. I remember my father often saying to a very young me that the Devil finds work for idle hands to do – which I took very seriously as a child, though it was a bit rich coming from a man who was not noted for energy and hard graft. A sort of shame about 'doing nothing' became ingrained, a fear of what my energetic mother called laziness.[42]

---

[42]   Laziness can be a facet of that sin the mediaevals called *accidia* and we English call Sloth, and reduce to something as banal as simply not getting up in the morning. But *Accidia* is far more deadly than simply having a lie-in. It is thinking that nothing really matters; the theologians said it was an unwillingness to seek the Lord while he might be found, and it can be very *busy* indeed with all the noise and bustle that stops you having time or energy to stop, think, contemplate. (I know it so, so well.) They also pointed out that reason, working things out, could so easily preclude contemplation, and the understanding, *intellectus*, which comes from it: like knowing how many bricks there are in the building and not seeing what it looks like or is for. Dickens put it better in his story in *Hard Times* (1854) of Mr Gradgrind questioning Girl Number Twenty, aka Sissy Jupes, on what a horse was.

CROSSROAD

When I was first earning my living in my first permanent job, there were two men older than me (both became close friends) whose example was – well, looking back, I am not sure it was wholly benign. For they would come home from work, and almost immediately take up some major project on which they were working – the next book, a paper to be written, a piece of slate to be lettered, a piece of fine hand letterpress printing to be done. I admired Martin and Brian, and felt theirs was an example of how life ought to be, brim-full and overflowing. 'Must get on with some work' – I can hear Brian's voice now as he finished his arrival-home cup of tea. But I do owe them a huge positive debt: they showed me so powerfully that life, even humdrum daily life, could be so *interesting*. I had never noticed typefaces, the texture of paper, or new letters cut into green, aeons-old Honister slate, or buff York sandstone, before I met Brian; I had never taken the trouble to look at the delicacy of yarrow leaves or the reciprocating spirals on the yellow centre of the daisy at my feet before I got to know Martin. And the tree grows the way the sapling bends with the winds. I used glibly to say to people, as if it were wisdom, 'If your holiday has been a good one, you should come back more tired than you went.' It can't have been much fun for the family.

Idle thoughts ... the word would not go away. That verse in Psalm 95 which warns that those who will not heed the Lord's voice 'shall not enter into my rest' – I say it every Matins – what does it *mean*? I don't think I'd ever really thought about it before: do the previous verses refer to the disobedient Israelites on their desert journey, who will not enter the Promised Land? That answer seems the view of

Hebrews 4: 9-11: a sabbath.[43] So, fidgeting, I looked up the word (isn't it wonderful you can do this with the internet, even in a storm?) in the Vulgate: *requies*. That word has at its root the idea of peace – it is etymologically connected with *civis,* a citizen, who may be presumed to be at peace and safe in his city. The Greek κατάπαυσις –

'ὡς ὤμοσα ἐν τῇ ὀργῇ μου εἰ εἰσελεύσονται
εἰς τὴν κατάπαυσίν μου' –

which is what the Greek has – means 'a putting to rest, a calming of the winds, a resting place', translating the Hebrew יְתָחֻנְּמ: – metaphorically the heavenly blessedness in which God dwells, which – I guess, humbly, with utter diffidence – from the Seventh Day *in saecula saeculorum* is an overwhelming Joy in Love for what He has made. (And here is the eternal problem: all those awe-ful things that lie at the very heart we can only grasp, visualise, through a metaphor that can so easily be mistaken for that which it is meant to reveal.)

But *requies,* κατάπαυσις, is surely more than just not working, for it also carries the idea of silence, even being silenced. In silence you can hear other people speak. Being at rest… be silent. The Orthodox Church has a tradition of hesychasm, of utterly silent prayer few of us in the talkative West know. Yet we have been told how important it is more than once: 'Be still, and know', as Psalm 46 puts it. Make space for our time-bound minds to intersect with no-time, in a moment when past and present and future cease

[43]   There remaineth therefore a sabbath rest for the people of God … Let us therefore give diligence to enter into that rest, that no man fall after the same example of [Israel's] disobedience.'

to have meaning, when stillness and movement are as one. The mathematical point at the centre of the globe has no dimension or movement, yet on it depends all the figure circumscribes, all its space and time. Maybe true rest is a dynamism, an equilibrium as powerful, balanced, silent, as the top spinning on its axis, perfectly at rest in its energy. Perhaps you can learn, perhaps you can be receptive, be – let's put the overworked word 'recreation', as in the 'R&R' given to soldiers after battle - into a verbal, passive, rather than a nominal form – 're-created.' But that means going back to the very Beginning, to the roots… If only, one sometimes wishes, we could go back and do it differently.[44]

Yes. Undo the grain in the wood twisted by the way the tree has grown. I have a lot to learn, and unlearn. In silence and stillness to recognise the goodness of all Creation, to let go – ('and then add a -d, and let God', as someone once said to me).

'Is it time yet for a gin?' my Beloved said. The rain was still lashing down, and had clearly set in for the night.

+ + +

[44]   After I wrote this, my friend Fr Philip Seddon told me of Bishop Simon Barrington-Ward, who had taught him, writing of going to the crypt of the Church of the Nativity in Bethlehem: 'I was overwhelmed by uncontrollable and unstoppable tears. And the phrase that welled up with the tears, and kept being repeated within me, was, 'If only we could begin all over again… If only we could begin all over again! What a mess we had made of it all! If only we could begin all over again.' In the end, quite quietly, gently and insistently, at last a voice seemed to respond, 'But you can, you can begin all over again, 'That is why I came. It was for this that I was born.' Stumbling back up the steps out of there afterwards, I somehow knew that this central theme of breaking and re-making was the pattern of our pilgrimage into the divine love, and always had been!' ('Simon's Orthodox Path A Rondo', in *Exchange of Gifts: The Vision of Simon Barrington-Ward*, eds. Graham Kings and Ian Randall, Edinburgh: Ekklesia Publishing 2022, in the Press.)

The smell of death, corruption, rotting, was what we noticed first as we rounded the low headland at the north of the island. We were walking west into a stiff wind from the bay they call now the White Strand of the Monks. Once, some time ago, skeins of seaweed, now dry, black, leathery, had accompanied the corpse to the high water mark of a storm. The sand had been blown, banked up against the jetsam, and grain by grain we could see the new dune building. Before very long it would cover the mass where it lay against the rocks shouldering out of the blown sand, but as yet some bones of the rib cage let the wind play through them, a grotesque silent harp. Tiny strips of flesh still clung, dried, dark red, black, to the bones. The orca cannot have been quite full grown, and the storm had thrown its carcase hard against the unyielding body of the island. How did it die? Difficult to say. But hard, perhaps – and it certainly felt pain, and knew it, and knew fear, for they are intelligent creatures. Its back was broken. Its flesh had been meat, the stuff of life, for scavengers of sea and air and earth.

A cloud had passed over our till then glibly cheerful morning, both of us in a sunny mood. The wind suddenly felt chill, and imagining what the pain of our fellow creature must have been made my mind flick back to the horror of that dying foal on Holy Island, and to another much earlier time, to the pungent, ammoniacal smell of the rotting cartilaginous spine of a basking shark on the beach stones of Arran. The dog had found it first, round the headland ahead of our walk, and had delightedly rolled on it before we could stop him. I had to explain to the two young children that this repellent mass was a relative of the huge basking shark whose leisurely fin the previous day they had seen cutting the water as the beast gently made its way along the coast, minding its own slow business.

Death, and killing, is everywhere woven into the weft of this life. I myself have killed, for I too am a predator, and as I shall die, I too will be food. My teeth show my species evolved as carnivores. But every time I bring down a pheasant or duck or pigeon, or land a fish, I thank it, and apologise to it, and feel a sadness that something beautiful, uniquely Itself, has left the world – all this, despite the joy and skill of the successful hunt. Alexander Pope knew exactly the contradictoriness of what I feel:

> See! from the brake the whirring pheasant springs,
> And mounts exulting on triumphant wings:
> Short is his joy; he feels the fiery wound,
> Flutters in blood, and panting beats the ground.
> Ah! what avail his glossy, varying dyes,
> His purple crest, and scarlet-circled eyes,
> The vivid green his shining plumes unfold,
> His painted wings, and breast that flames with gold?

Something paradoxical, and very old, stirs in me whenever I kill for the pot. I am sure our hunter-gatherer forebears knew that bond between quarry and hunter that the Inuit, for example, acknowledge, recognising the seal or bear or caribou as being as much a person as they are. They love and honour it, and what they have killed will be reborn. That feeling seems very close sometimes – almost as if you want not simply to *have* the quarry, but to *be* it, to share its life, its way of seeing. Is that what the shamans, like the Noaidis of the Sámi – I have met a woman who claims to be one – are able to do? What a gift that would be! Our prey deserves honour, respect, whether it be the bullock I have met several times nicely putting on weight down the lane from where I write, or the lean wild geese flying in on the winter wind. It is still even now customary in some countries, like Poland, Germany, France, and others, where old manners survive, to salute the quarry, to accord it respect, to give it thanks.[45]

The dead whale on that sunny windy morning reminds that even in our mental Arcadias, there Death, pain, is too, never far away … *Et in Arcadia ego* … The hard truth presses in once more, that dying is what we are made for, born to do. By it, however remotely, we enable other creatures to live. Opposites cleave to each other in a bond of universal love, self-giving – only we lament, we howl, for ourselves and all we love, for we have lost the eyes to see that truth, and the ears to hear the holding of the voices in a cosmic harmony of endless giving and receiving, receiving and giving. Remember, O man, that dust thou art and to dust thou shalt return. May mine be fertile.

Later that day the rain came again in from the west, really hard. We went out, of course. At the north end of the island we sat with our back to the wet wind against the miniature cliff where the dunes ended and the sea reached – an appropriately

[45] Our mediaeval ancestors, as they encouraged the boar, a big, fast, dangerous animal indeed, a worthy adversary, to charge to meet the sword or spear thrust of the Lord of the Hunt, would respectfully call him 'Mestre', and in France the curling horns still sound their melancholy note through the woods as he lies new dead. The fallen stag is saluted by the horns blowing the mort before his carcase is loaded into the pickup. *J'aime, le soir, le son du Cor au fond des bois* – I learned Alfred de Vigny's poem at school, and had no idea then what he was talking about. But that sombre sound called in the dogs, and marked the ritual respect for the fellow creature whose life had been given for the food of men.

in-between place for the day before we would have to step back into everyday with whatever we could carry from here for the next leg of the journey. I don't know what she thought: I was seeing dear dead Hector running and playing happily at the edge of the tide, trying to bite the waves and shaking his head at the taste of the salt, and the first time we had sat here, years ago, and

> Like sepulchral statues lay;
> All day, the same our postures were,
> And we said nothing, all the day.

Joy remembered is still joy. A couple came round the corner onto the white strand, and at first did not see us. She was barefoot and carrying her sandals, he whipcord tough in bare legs and heavy mountain boots. As happens sometimes, something in the way greetings were exchanged led to liking, desultory conversation. They knew the little wheelhead cross painted on the rocks, which we had found on our first visit to this strand: another place where Vikings on one of their slaving raids had slaughtered the monks they could not cram into their ship. That cross seems so hidden, so much 'ours' – for beneath it, some of my ashes one day will be scattered. As conversation accelerated and deepened, it was clear, in an unspoken understanding, that they came for the same reasons we did, which none of us talked of. We shall never see them again.

Off the shore of this wonderful wilderness is where the two tidal streams, the eastern and the western, round the island meet and their waters join in waves that dance obliquely into each other and explode in a joy of spray with which the winds play. (Just as our two lives have come together ...) It was once the island's dump, the man had said. His mother – so he came here as a child! – would never let her family come to the north end for that reason. So all the rubbish lies here, under the machair and the dunes where the sheep graze. This is Iona's Vale of Hinnom … Yet time … The sands, the little dunes, have covered the white strand where the blood the Norsemen shed reddened the edge of the tide,[46] they have covered what people no longer value or want, the broken things, as they are covering the dead whale. One day, even, aeons hence, the sand will have hardened into stone, and the whale may be a fossil.

✦ ✦ ✦

Iona – well, superficially it is still the nondescript sort of place it was when I first went there. Its rocks remain when our earthly selves shall be merely a memory. Shaping those selves may be what it's all about. For if you will only listen, be still, Iona is a place of energy, palpable, pulsing out into the world that so needs the healing and reconciliation it can engender. To get on the early ferry to come back to a *less* real world of busy-ness and imperative irrelevance is always hard. Yet, though too soon return always is, oddly, it *is* soon enough, for something imperious says there *is* work to do, the hands must not be idle. Go and tell the story as best you can.

---

[46] Vikings were good businessmen. There was a ready domestic and foreign market for slaves, if you could get them to it. Furthermore, though they were mainly pagan until around 1000, they also knew there was a ready market among Christians for relics of the saints and martyrs. When a raiding party murdered Blathmac at the steps of the altar in the Abbey, they were trying to force him to reveal where Columba's relics were. That was what they were after, and they must have done their homework. Slaughter was merely incidental, merely collateral damage.

We took the ferry back, picked up the car. But on the way down to the house by the Fen ...

South of Berwick, a traffic light halted us at a crossroad. To the left, Aidan's, and Cuthbert's, Lindisfarne, called. After all, why not? Iona had trained Aidan. King Oswald summoned him thence to spearhead the conversion of Northumbria. That wise king, who had abandoned the old gods and been baptised in Iona, gave him the island of Lindisfarne,[47] within sight of the royal seat at Bamburgh and near the great royal hall of Yeavering. So: start the excursion to recalibrate the imperatives with a trip to one holy island, and top it up with a bonus trip to another.

The weather could hardly have been more different from our daily sousing on Iona: balmy sun, hordes of people in holiday mood and undress, their cars making the causeway across the sands – only safe at low tide – noisy and hazardous. In contrast, a few barelegged people made their muddy way across the sands by the old pilgrim route. We stopped by the first big dunes, initially for personal reasons, but stayed because of the host of seals happily hauled out on the sandbank across the channel and the myriad wading birds calling. We stood there with our binoculars, quietly rejoicing, and a car coming off the island drew up beside ours. A couple got out. A smile. That sort of instant liking: as if to say, 'We have known and understood each other a long time.' 'What are you watching?' 'The seals – and those redshanks by the water.' They stood, rapt like ourselves. Too soon stopped time resumed, and she said, 'We have a long way to go, to Wells.' And I said, 'So do we, to Cambridge, but we would not miss this.' It was uncertain what 'this' was. 'No,' he said, 'No, we would not

---

[47] Curiously, the name means 'Island of the travellers from or to Lindsey', i.e. the area round Lincoln.

either.' And our ways parted. But such moments are the glimpses of joy we are allowed.

We put the binoculars away and got back in the car. By the large car park on the island, an ice-cream van and a seafood stall were busy, with queues of people in guzzly holiday mood. On the road into the village, two stalls selling vegetable and other produce were, to judge from the large emphatic notice one had set up, engaged in a bitter turf war. The pubs were doing excellent trade. A regular procession of people made their way to the castle which Edward Hudson, the founder of *Country Life* ('incorporating *Racing Illustrated*') bought in 1897, and had Lutyens restore. The garden Gertrude Jekyll had made was popular.

We walked along the shallow curve of the beach towards the present harbour. Quite clearly, once upon a time the sea had reached further inland, where now sheep and cattle may safely graze. It must have been here that the bows of the tarred black boats of that first Viking raid in 793 bit the shingle. Alcuin of York, writing from Charlemagne's court in Aachen to his friend Higbald, Lindisfarne's bishop, saw the raid as a portent, a complete shock, as judgement of God on a backsliding people. They 'desecrated God's sanctuaries, and poured the blood of saints within the compass of the altar, destroyed the house of our hope, trampled the bodies of saints in God's temple like animal dung in the street ...'. The *Anglo Saxon Chronicle* says something similar with the same air of shock. We are so used to seeing that raid as the first shower of the long storm that convulsed Europe for three hundred years. But I think we forget that the men of the North had been visiting Britain and trading for time out of mind: they and their fast ships were well known, even welcome.

Even at the height of the crisis of Alfred's reign 70 or so years later, that wise king was happily chatting to Ottar, a rich and powerful visitor from north Norway to his court, and making notes on what he told him. The most terrible thing about the raid – all the early raids – is that probably the ships were seen in the offing and nobody thought anything about it. After all, trade with these people, and eating and drinking with them, was quite normal. But when they turn on you … you think of neighbours you have known all your life suddenly becoming inexplicably dangerous, hostile, murderous … poor Ireland in both sets of Troubles, Germany in the 1930s …

Dark thoughts on a lovely day with the sun edging the wavelets with spectral glory. The walk along the harbour was problematic because 'social distancing' (should it not be '*anti-social*'?) was not easy along the narrow path. (Some sort of parable there?) In the museum, informative notices had a polite subtext that implied, alas perhaps rightly, that most readers would not be, shall we say, of the Faith. The ruins of the Priory – well, there are traces on the wind-eroded sandstone piers of the nave that show it had been a sort of miniature Durham Cathedral, and the so-called Rainbow Arch – actually once one of the two crossing ribs of the vault under the tower – was skeletally stupendous against the sky, but … seen one Benedictine ruin, seen 'em all. When the Priory was suppressed it was used to store the naval stores Henry VIII's captains needed in their watch against the troublesome Scots. A few years later, the fort – the Castle – was made using the Priory as a stone quarry. Nothing here for the spirit save a reminder of 'the distress that we are in, how Jerusalem lieth waste, and the gates thereof are burned with fire.'

Impatience and irritation mounted. Then we said, 'Let us arise, and go to the islet where St Cuthbert built his first solitude.' At low tide you can walk to Hobthrush Island. Indeed, Cuthbert soon realized it was too close to Lindisfarne; monks could shout over to him even when the tide was in. So he left, for Inner Farne, where no one before him had ever stayed for long.

Any structure Cuthbert might have used would of course have been wooden, and no visible trace remains of that. There are only the lowest stone courses of a later oratory, or hermitage. But even so that short way across the sand, across the multitude of broken shells, slipping on the bladder wrack growing on the exposed knobs of the black whinstone that a volcano aeons ago spewed out, was liminal. A few people, a little group with a priest, stood with their backs to the big wooden cross marking the oratory, binoculars at the ready, watching a few swimming seals: they had not noticed the 500 or so on the big sandbank across the water, hauled out for a refreshing rest from guzzling fish. A rectangle, 10 feet by eight or so, of worked stone marked the foundations of the oratory, and next to it the remnants of a cell. Beneath the big wooden cross were placed little offerings: a few coins, dull with weather, a pattern of shells, and a three inch stone with on it, in white paint, 'I am Alpha and Omega, the First and the Last.' I sat down on the broken wall. A woman sitting further along, obviously at prayer, looked up and smiled: recognition. Rosanna came and sat beside me. 'It's about time,' she said, 'so we might as well.' So we said the Angelus together, not quite daring to sing it. And sat for a while in silence, thinking our thoughts – is that prayer? – here, on the spot where Cuthbert had prayed and meditated. This is what we came here for. Carried on the wind we could hear the seals on the sandbank singing. Or singing, anyway.

Less is after all more. If only one could keep that in mind … (perhaps even when writing.) but it became, as usual, a memory of a difference, as we made our way down the busy A1 to 'normal', through the thickening soup of lorries in a hurry, coagulating at junctions. Eventually, the last lap, the acres upon acres of the new A14, which in its building had obliterated henge and burial, farm and droveway, that the old ones had left. ('Your A14', the signs tell us, as they remind us that they are 'Working for You Even Out of View' – so kind.)

And so back to The News, to the stupendous irrelevance of the things that so many of us measure our lives by, to being reminded of the serial dishonesty and lack of honour in the current shower ruling us, to the refusal of the really powerful to face the really big issue that makes all politics and business laughable, that imminent, inevitable, catastrophic change in climate that will engulf them as well as everyone else. They have stolen our dreams, indeed, as the excellent and brave Greta Thunberg said. But Iona is one of those places where I think I have glimpsed the deep truth of those ancient words of Lady Julian, writing in her cell in Norwich nearly six centuries ago, when in another time of General Crisis, drastic worsening of climate, inexplicable plague, war and sudden death stalked her world: 'All shall be well, all shall be well, all manner of thing shall be well'. We may not understand how, but that does not mean she was wrong. Hold fast to that. For the darkness does not comprehend the light. Just let us lift our eyes from the mud our feet are – o so comfortably! – stuck in, where 'we know what we have got to deal with', and see the sunlight lighting up the distant hills, as I saw for the first time the Sunlit Uplands of the Lake District from the summit of The Helm all those years ago. There are other journeys, all one Journey, to be done. Emmaus may be closer than we think.

8

... To Seek a Newer World

The Master Of The Caravan:
But who are ye in rags and rotten shoes,
You dirty-bearded, blocking up the way?
The Pilgrims:
We are the Pilgrims, master; we shall go
Always a little further: it may be
Beyond the last blue mountain barred with snow,
Across that angry or that glimmering sea,
White on a throne or guarded in a cave
There lives a prophet who can understand
Why men were born: but surely we are brave,
Who take the golden road to Samarkand.
The Chief Merchant:
We gnaw the nail of hurry. Master, away!

James Elroy Flecker, *Hassan* (1913)

Here I am, an old man in a dry month ... and stirred, as ever, by restlessness. I am aware that there is unfinished business and that time does not get more ample. What to do? I could not see how to end this endless book. My Lady gave good advice: 'Feature the problem. Be open about it.' So I shall. I have been telling, and thinking about, a story, and I do not know its end, for I think there is something essential that we can only know by dying. And then of course we can't tell it. We really don't know what life is, what it is about, until we know what death is, just as we do not know how good a book is until we close it after the last page and it makes a whole shape.

But do stories ever end? There can be no conclusion as long as the journeys keep unfolding from each other. When I was very young, and first discovering with utter, totally unscholarly, delight the 'wide expanse ... That deep-brow'd Homer ruled as his demesne', his story of Odysseus' search for home and peace captivated me, and it has done ever since. But the warning Teiresias gave him was sombre: there could be no rest, no abiding city in the Ithaca he called home, for the past bears too heavily on the present. He must leave, find a place where he and his prowess were unknown, where the people do not know his story, or even of the wine dark seas he had sailed, where he was just – an unaccommodated man: the first word of the poem, as it happens, in the Greek. Nothing else. When all is stripped away, what is left? All those things we trust in, all the achievements and glory and possessions we strive for when our life is climbing to its noon ... and then the sunset nears and physical powers decline; brain and memory slow, weaken; eyesight clouds; reputation – well, generations come that know not Joseph; achievement: St Thomas Aquinas, as his life drew to its end, said his massive, world-changing, work reminded him of so much straw; families grow away into their own stories; friends die – as Henry Vaughan put it, 'They are all gone into a world of light! / And I alone sit ling'ring here.' Odysseus has – we have – to be known for what he simply had made himself, ἀρετή without any κλέος or kudos. What he added up to has to be faced ... and only then will he have peace, untroubled by the tides of Poseidon's sea.

The cocksureness of youth, of mid-career, with which I would once announce my thinking, has gone, and I am older, humbled by failures, rejections, human suffering, study, and the sophistications, *chiaroscuro,* as well as the unexpected joys, of experience. Do I now know more or less? Do I understand better? I am really not sure; what I am sure about is that the Story is too big for our little minds to grasp all at once, that any statement we make must be provisional, that radical doubt of our temporary certainties is how we grow. We evolve by the trial and error of natural selection: why should we think some similar rule does not apply to our individual and corporate understanding? And sometimes, in certain places, certain events and situations, we do glimpse things that seem to lie at the very heart of the mystery, out of time, to feel things so strongly that sometimes the hairs on the back of your neck rise. That feeling is real, water in the thirsty desert, signposts to where we would be: at Home. It is important on the unknown road to the unknown place to turn to a fellow traveller, like that man on the lonely Norfolk road, that couple on Iona, or the couple from Wells on Lindisfarne, and to say, 'Did you see that? You, too?' For if I have learned one thing, it is that we are constantly surrounded, nudged, by reminders that we are members one of another, starlings of the same unending murmuration. We inherit the experience of the past only to build on it as our small part in the music of Creation.

The pilgrimage of this book, which is both journey and the

writing of journeys, is not over. I have often asked myself, both in the travelling and in its retrospect, what it might add up to. Up on The Helm that small boy I once knew wanted to go higher and further, to achieve more and more. But now … He had to learn that the way down the hill into the ordinariness of everyday matters too, for there were people, one in especial, waiting for him. There is no point in seeking, in pilgrimage or retreat, the grace of a new understanding or insight, a recalibration, if it simply stops there. That would, in the end, be simply self-indulgent. The experience has to spread out, as ripples from a pebble in a pond, or the pattern of deflected waves round an island. The news from nowhere has to work like yeast, in the life we lead, the way we treat each other, our animals, our plants, the very soils we take for granted yet without which we are all dead. It has to affect the way we acknowledge, and act, our *creaturlich* status.

We are all God's hands in His world, and there is work to do. That world is palpably in desperate need of healing. It is utterly plain there is nothing but cataclysmic disaster ahead if we keep doing the same things that got us here in the first place. It is essential that we as individuals, as societies, as cultures, root out the false dichotomy that separates 'material' and 'spiritual', that we reconnect the apparent opposites of yin and yang, male and female, in a unity that depends on but subsumes both. This is a journey to the heart, to recognise that we are in a Web of life where everything affects everything else, where everything depends on, is responsible in its measure, for everything else. We cannot stand aside from this 'everything else', for we are of it.

I look at the intricate interlace designs of the Book of Kells (which may well have originated in Iona) or the Lindisfarne

Gospels, at the arabesque and geometric styles of Islamic art, at polyphony in late mediaeval Western music, at the narrative form of some of the great mediaeval romances, and cannot help wondering if ideologically they are all based on an apprehension of the interdependence of everything. God loves *all* things into Being, all have their source in him. Each one of us, each creature from subatomic particle (and we may be sure that that is not the end of *that* story) to rocks, to animate things, reflects in our measure the wholeness and harmony we can observe in the patterns in the whole universe, pattern in almost musical form in holons and fractals.

✦ ✦ ✦

I was weary when I started to write this epilogue – after all, as the Preacher said, of the making of books there is no end and much study is a weariness of the flesh – but writing it has been like the sound of the trumpet to the warhorse, even if pawing in the valley is now beyond me. The wound of desire, that delicious pain, summons. Come, my friends,

> 'Tis not too late to seek a newer world ...
> Tho' much is taken, much abides; and tho'
> We are not now that strength which in old days
> Moved earth and heaven, that which we are, we are.
>
> Tennyson, *Ulysses* (1842)

The next journey calls: 'I have a journey, sir, shortly to go. My master calls me; I must not say no.' A friend of mine walked, despite *angina pectoris,* to Santiago; my Lady walked a silent retreat high in the Asturias hills; two friends of mine, on his retirement from the Navy, walked the Via Francigena from Canterbury to Rome (her only regret was that she only took one bra for a three month walk ...). I must arise and go now ... The road to heaven starts at our door, and the time is now. In the end it may be that simply walking the rolling English roads, which is all I may be able to do, will lead us to

> walk with clearer eyes and ears this path that wandereth,
> And see undrugged in evening light the decent inn of death;
> For there is good news yet to hear and fine things to be seen,
> Before we go to Paradise by way of Kensal Green.

One root meaning of the word 'Salvation' is healing, healing for that wound of desire. Is that what Rest is? And the answer to that but half suspected desire, as good Richard Hooker calls it, may be staring you in the Faith.